Ian MacDonald

ESSENTIALS

GCSE Design & Technology
Product Design
Workbook

Contents

Contents

Processing Materials

Exam-style Questions

History of Product Design

Design Movements

1 Which of the following statements describe influences on product design? Tick the **three** correct options.

- **A** The discovery of new materials ☑
- **B** Manufacturing and technological developments ☑
- **C** Climate changes ☐
- **D** Changes in political party leaders ☐
- **E** Fashions, trends and the latest thinking ☑

Influences of Nature

2 Circle the correct options in the following sentences.

a) The **Art Nouveau / Arts and Crafts Movement** was founded by William Morris and was inspired by natural patterns and forms.

b) The **Art Nouveau / Arts and Crafts Movement** included designers like Charles Rennie Mackintosh, and was based on natural, organic lines.

Influences of Industry

3 The table contains the names of four design movements.

Match descriptions **A**, **B**, **C** and **D** with the movements **1–4** in the table. Enter the appropriate number in the boxes provided.

	Movement
1	Bauhaus
2	De Stijl
3	Modernist
4	Art Deco

- **A** Influenced by industrialised designs and made use of geometric shapes ☐
- **B** A German school of art and design that produced early designs for mass production ☐
- **C** Started in Holland and featured extreme geometric designs ☐
- **D** Influenced by artefacts in Tutankhamen's recently opened tomb ☐

4 Which art movement were Piet Mondrian and Gerrit Rietveld associated with? Tick the correct option.

- **A** Bauhaus ☐
- **B** Art Deco ☐
- **C** De Stijl ☐
- **D** Modernist ☐

History of Product Design

War, Post-war and the 1960s

1 Choose the correct words from the options given to complete the following sentences.

speed **science** **consumers** **materials** **cheaply** **icons** **transport**

The streamlined age was about .... and movement. New ....

and production methods allowed designs to be manufactured ....

There were three main influences: the rapid growth in .... design, the interest in

.... and the race to put the first man on the Moon.

2 What design icon is Alec Issigonis best known for? Tick the correct option.

A Mini skirt ☐ **B** Mini mouse ☐

C Mini chocolate bar ☐ **D** Mini Morris ☐

3 What design icon is Mary Quant best known for? Tick the correct option.

A Mini skirt ☐ **B** Mini mouse ☐

C Mini chocolate bar ☐ **D** Mini Morris ☐

1970–Present Day

4 Circle the correct option in the following sentence.

By the 1980s, brand was increasingly important to consumers. The **client / user / manufacturer / designer** label spread from fashion markets to other areas of product design.

5 What group was Ettore Sottsass associated with? Tick the correct option.

A Blobist Group ☐ **B** Modernist Group ☐

C Art Deco Group ☐ **D** Memphis Group ☐

6 Choose the correct words from the options given to complete the following sentences.

CAD **straight** **CAM** **flowing** **curved**

Blobjects is a current trend characterised by a lack of .... lines, and produced in a variety of ways. The development of sophisticated .... software has allowed complex .... forms to be designed and manufactured.

Classic and Retro Designs

Design Icons

1 Why might a design be considered 'iconic'? Tick the **three** correct options.

- **A** Because of the way that technology has been used
- **B** Because it uses electronic components
- **C** Because it uses clever and innovate styling
- **D** Because it appeals only to wealthy people
- **E** Because it simply has a 'must own' quality

Some Classic Designs

2 Explain why the Coca-cola bottle is considered to be an iconic design.

....

....

3 Circle the correct options in the following sentences.

a) Marcel Breuer's **Juicy Salif lemon squeezer / Wassily Chair**, designed in 1925, was apparently inspired by a bicycle frame and uses the Bauhaus principles of form following function.

b) Philippe Starck's **Salif lemon squeezer / Wassily Chair** was very controversial with critics saying it was extravagant and unpractical.

Retro Styling

4 In which of the following design styles is retro styling commonly seen? Tick the correct option.

- **A** Where there's an influence from ancient Rome
- **B** Where there's an influence from ancient Egypt
- **C** Where there's an influence from about 40 years ago
- **D** Where there's an influence from medieval design

5 Which of the following objects represent a retro design? Tick the **two** correct options.

- **A** Biro pen
- **B** DeLonghi toaster
- **C** London Underground map
- **D** Chrysler PT Cruiser

Market Pull and Technological Push

Market Pull

1 Choose the correct words from the options given to complete the following sentences.

increased **product** **market place** **decreased** **development** **idea** **create**

The .... creates consumer demand. Consumers see a ....

that they want to buy. This creates a demand for the product and can often lead to

.... and expansion of that product.

Manufacturers can help to .... consumer demand, for example with the Sony Walkman in the late 1970s. The technology had been around for some time, but consumer demand suddenly .... when Sony developed a product for people to listen to music whilst on the move.

Technological Push

2 Which of the following statements describe **technological push**? Tick the **two** correct options.

- **A** The technological advance of new materials ☐
- **B** The technological decision to make fewer products ☐
- **C** The technological decision to make larger products ☐
- **D** The technological advance of production methods ☐

3 Choose the correct words from the options given to complete the following sentences.

Teflon **heat-tolerant** **water-resistant** **physicist** **space satellites** **chemist**

Tetrafluoroethylene resin, otherwise known as ...., was first discovered whilst a chemist was researching refrigerants. This new material is very .... and stick-resistant. The coating of this material has been used on .... and non-stick pans.

4 How were microwave ovens developed? Tick the correct option.

- **A** From First World War tank technology ☐
- **B** From Second World War RADAR technology ☐
- **C** From Cold War battle technology ☐
- **D** From space technology ☐

Continuous Improvement

Quality Control Guidelines

1 What does TQM stand for?

2 What is BS EN ISO 9000:2005? Tick the correct option.

- **A** Guidelines by which companies are assessed
- **B** Guidelines that companies set for their products
- **C** Guidelines by which government organisations are assessed
- **D** Guidelines by which employees are assessed

3 How does BS EN ISO 9000:2005 help / protect consumers?

4 Which of the following statements describe how BS EN ISO 9000:2005 is applied? Tick the **two** correct options.

- **A** It's time spent looking at ways to avoid paying tax
- **B** It's time spent looking at how to make more money
- **C** It's time spent looking at how to improve products or manufacturing methods
- **D** It's time spent looking at the way products work

5 What are **standard controls**?

6 What are **quality circles**?

7 Choose the correct words from the options given to complete the following sentences.

workforce **simple** **complicated** **manufacturing** **procedures**

When dealing with a .... product, e.g. a car, the process of producing the product can become very complex. For example, the .... may be in different parts of a country, or even in different countries. Every part of a product is specified and documented. There are set .... to follow if anyone thinks there is a problem with a product.

Product Evolution

Why Products Evolve

1 Which of the following statements describe valid reasons for products evolving over time? Tick the **two** correct options.

- **A** Cost of living changes ☐
- **B** New technologies ☐
- **C** Changes in manufacturing ☐
- **D** Changes of government ☐

2 Match changes **A**, **B**, **C** and **D** with the results **1–4** in the table. Enter the appropriate number in the boxes provided.

- **A** Developments in new materials ☐
- **B** Changing fashions ☐
- **C** Changes in manufacturing methods ☐
- **D** Social changes ☐

	Results
1	Women going out to work
2	Automated production processes
3	Smart materials
4	Seasonal colours in textile products

Example of Product Evolution

3 The iron is an example of a product that has evolved over time.

Look at the images below and suggest **two** significant differences between the two irons.

Iron, 1900s

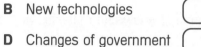

Modern-day Iron

a) ....

b) ....

4 The iron below, developed in the 1950s, has an adjustable plate temperature. Explain why an adjustable plate temperature would have been introduced.

....

....

Sustainability Issues

Effect on the Environment

1 Circle the correct options in the following sentences.

a) **Non-renewable / Renewable** materials are grown from plants or animals.

b) **Non-renewable / Renewable** materials are taken from oil, ores and minerals.

2 Choose from the options below to insert the correct description **1–4** into the table.

1 Waste and 'end of life' materials should be recycled rather than being put into landfill sites

2 Natural resources and energy costs will be saved and products will be cheaper for the consumer

3 Reduce the amount of raw materials used to manufacture products

4 Repair

Process	Description	Explanation
Reduce	A	Fewer natural resources will be used up and energy will also be saved
B	Products should be designed so that they can easily be repaired if they break	C ....
Recycle	D	This will reduce the amount of material in landfill sites and will reduce the use of raw materials

Recycling / Disposing of Products

3 Give two reasons why plastic is **not** considered to be environmentally friendly.

a) .... b) ....

4 Why does packaging have symbols on it? Tick the **two** correct options.

A To make the packaging look pretty ☐

B To identify materials that can be recycled ☐

C So we know how to dispose of certain materials ☐

D So we know what our rights as consumers are ☐

5 What does the following symbol mean?

.... ☐

Re-using Materials

1 Circle the correct options in the following sentences.

a) An old machine will be **recycled / re-used** if it's dismantled and the parts are used again.

b) An old machine will be **recycled / re-used** if it's melted down and the materials are used again.

2 Re-using products reduces the amount of processing needed. Why is this a benefit? Tick the **two** correct options.

A Products are easier to clean ☐ **B** Products are more environmentally friendly ☐

C Products are cheaper ☐ **D** Products look more attractive ☐

3 Give one example of a material / product that could be re-used.

Carbon Footprint and Product Miles

4 What unit is a carbon footprint measured in? Tick the correct option.

A Carbon ☐ **B** Carbon dioxide ☐

C Carbon trioxide ☐ **D** Carbonation ☐

5 What is the definition of **product miles**? Tick the correct option.

A The number of miles we travel everyday ☐

B The number of miles a product travels in its lifetime ☐

C The number of miles a product travels everyday ☐

D The number of miles a product travels from a shop to our home ☐

Product Life Cycles

6 Approximately what percentage of crude oil goes towards the manufacture of plastics? Tick the correct option.

A 1% ☐ **B** 7% ☐ **C** 30% ☐ **D** 90% ☐

7 In what three ways can plastics be disposed of / re-used at the end of their life?

a)

b)

c)

Packaging and Labelling

Packaging

1 The table contains the names of six materials that can be used for packaging.

Match descriptions **A**, **B**, **C**, **D**, **E** and **F** with the packaging features **1–6** in the table. Enter the appropriate number in the boxes provided.

A To make sure that a product arrives without damage ☐

B To give users knowledge about the product ☐

C To keep any loose materials or components together ☐

D To make sure that the product can be clearly seen ☐

E To stop factors such as the weather, temperature and bacteria from deteriorating the product ☐

F To allow the product to be moved easily from place to place ☐

	Material
1	Containing
2	Information
3	Preservation
4	Transportation
5	Protection
6	Display

Packaging Symbols

2 Which of the following statements describe valid reasons for using a bar code? Tick the **two** correct options.

A To allow shops to keep prices secret ☐

B To eliminate human error ☐

C To make it easier to prosecute under-age drinkers ☐

D Stock control ☐

3 Name two examples of maintenance, storage or handling symbols that you might find on packaging.

a) ....

b) ....

Food Labelling

4 Match descriptions **A**, **B**, **C** and **D** with the requirements **1–4** in the table. Enter the appropriate number in the boxes provided.

A Products can't be sold beyond this and should be thrown away once the date has passed ☐

B Details of the maker, packer or seller ☐

C All the ingredients must be listed in decreasing order of weight, including additives and preservatives ☐

D Particularly important after a food product has been opened ☐

	Requirements
1	Use by dates
2	Ingredients
3	Contact details
4	Storage instructions

Flat Pack Furniture

1 Give three reasons why consumers may prefer to buy flat pack furniture.

a) ....

b) ....

c) ....

2 Give three reasons why manufacturers may prefer to build flat pack furniture.

a) ....

b) ....

c) ....

3 What kind of fittings are often used for flat pack furniture? Tick the correct option.

- **A** Rivets ☐
- **B** Knock-up fittings ☐
- **C** Knock-down fittings ☐
- **D** Reinforced concrete bars ☐

Assembly and Instruction Booklets

4 Which of the following statements describe valid reasons for having a well-designed assembly and instruction booklet? Tick the **two** correct options.

- **A** It tells the consumer where to buy spare parts ☐
- **B** It tells the consumer how much they have saved ☐
- **C** It tells the consumer how to assemble the product ☐
- **D** It tells the consumer how to use the product ☐

5 Why do assembly and instruction booklets rely on graphics? Tick the correct option.

- **A** The graphics make the product more interesting to assemble ☐
- **B** It makes the booklets look more attractive ☐
- **C** It's cheaper to produce ☐
- **D** Graphics can be used to overcome language barriers ☐

Product Maintenance

Product Maintenance

1 Choose the correct words from the options given to complete the following sentences.

maintenance **expectancy** **warranty** **style** **batteries**

Many products have a life .... based on some degree of maintenance, e.g. simple products like personal stereos need to have the .... changed regularly. Complex products, e.g. cars, have very detailed .... schedules.

Symbols

2 Why is it important that there is an international code for clothing manufacturers?

....

3 Explain what the following product maintenance symbols mean.

a) ....

b) ....

c) ....

Designed Obsolescence

4 Choose the correct words from the options given to complete the following sentences.

thrown away **are** **convenient** **room** **raw materials** **aren't** **accidentally** **deliberately**

Planned obsolescence is when a product has been .... designed to be .... after a certain period of time, e,g. disposal razors and cameras. These products are often .... to use, but they can use up the same amounts of .... and energy as more long-lasting products. They .... environmentally friendly.

Product Maintenance and Human Factors

Standard Components

1. Which of the following statements describe valid reasons for using standard components? Tick the **two** correct options.

   A It's easy to replace components ☐
   B Products can be repaired easily ☐
   C It makes a product more environmentally friendly ☐
   D It makes a product more reliable ☐

Human Factors

2. Which of the following statements is **not** a factor that needs to be considered when designing a product for humans? Tick the correct option.

   A Physiological factors ☐ **B** Metrological factors ☐
   C Psychological factors ☐ **D** Sociological factors ☐

Stereotypes

3. Circle the correct options in the following sentences.

   a) A target **market / user** is a person who may want to buy or use the product being sold.

   b) A target **market / user** is a group of people who may want to buy or use the product being sold.

Inclusive and Exclusive Design

4. Choose the correct words from the options given to complete the following sentences.

   exclude **inclusive design** **responsibility** **careful designing** **entertain**

   The ideal product is one that meets everyone's needs. This is called .... and designers try to .... as few people as possible.

   Designers have a .... to make sure that nothing they design will offend the people who will use the products.

5. What is the difference between inclusive design and exclusive design?

   ....

   ....

Human Factors

Physiological Factors

1 Choose the correct words from the options given to complete the following sentences.

strength **physical** **weakness** **mental** **move**

Physiological factors are concerned with the .... limitations of people.

Although people tend to .... their bodies in similar ways and have similar hand / eye co-ordination, they do vary greatly in size, ... and levels of stamina.

Anthropometrics and Ergonomics

2 What is anthropometrics the study of?

....

....

3 What is ergonomics the study of?

....

....

4 Choose the correct words from the options given to complete the following sentences.

safety **hundreds** **80%** **comfort** **90%** **charts** **boxes** **45%** **millions**

Anthropometric data is measurements that have been taken from .... of people and put together in ....

Designers try to cater for .... of the population and use this data to deal with issues such as .... and ....

Human Factors

Working Triangles

1 What is the term **working triangle** used to describe?

2 Give two examples of situations in which a designer would use a working triangle.

a)

b)

3 What can a working triangle also be known as? Tick the correct option.

- **A** Reach letter ☐
- **B** Reach envelope ☐
- **C** Reach paper ☐
- **D** Reach note ☐

Adjustment

4 Which of the following products often need to be adjustable? Tick the **two** correct options.

- **A** Bicycles ☐
- **B** Garden seats ☐
- **C** Hammer handles ☐
- **D** Office chairs ☐

Psychological Factors

5 What are psychological factors concerned with? Tick the correct option.

- **A** How the body works ☐
- **B** How the brain works ☐
- **C** How we move ☐
- **D** How we grow and develop ☐

6 Why is it important that designers understand about psychological factors when designing products?

Touch, Taste and Smell

7 The table contains the names of three senses that are important factors when looking at products.

Match examples of products **A**, **B** and **C** with the senses **1–3** in the table.
Enter the appropriate number in the boxes provided.

- **A** Toothpaste and lip gloss ☐
- **B** Textured upholstery and hot water bottles ☐
- **C** Lemon-scented toilet cleaner and lavender-scented bubble bath ☐

	Sense
1	Taste
2	Smell
3	Touch

Human Factors

Sound and Sight

1 What products rely on our sense of hearing to give a warning? Tick the **two** correct options.

A Warning lights ☐ **B** Fire alarms ☐

C Car horns ☐ **D** Vibrating phones ☐

2 The volume of noise is important. Explain what could be the danger in the following situations.

a) If a fire alarm is too quiet.

....

b) If a car horn is too loud.

....

3 What kind of visual information do people respond to? Tick the **two** correct options.

A Coloured signs ☐ **B** Hot radiators ☐

C Digital displays ☐ **D** The aroma of warm bread ☐

4 What colour would you expect a danger sign to be in? Tick the correct option.

A Red ☐ **B** Blue ☐ **C** Green ☐ **D** Brown ☐

5 Which of the following colours suggest cleanliness? Tick the **two** correct options.

A Purple ☐ **B** Blue ☐ **C** White ☐ **D** Brown ☐

Sociological Factors and Disability

6 Give **two** examples of sociological issues that are important in transport design and architecture.

a) ....

b) ....

7 Choose the correct words from the options given to complete the following sentences.

disability **mobility** **inclusive** **young** **public** **buildings** **transport**

For some people .... is a permanent feature of their lives. Designers must be fully aware of the needs of all areas of disability in order to make their products more .... This is particularly important for .... spaces and services.

Human Factors

Access

1 Why does putting graphic instructions on a product mean that it can be used by a wide range of people?

2 A child-proof lock on a fridge will stop a small child from opening it, but which other users might it also cause a problem for? Tick the **two** correct options.

A Athletes ☐ **B** The elderly ☐

C People with limited strength ☐ **D** Office workers ☐

Safety

3 The table contains three safety situations.

Match descriptions **A**, **B** and **C** with the situations **1–3** in the table. Enter the appropriate number in the boxes provided.

A To protect a user from a hot kettle ☐

B To stop a product being swallowed by a small child ☐

C To prevent a baby from getting their head stuck ☐

	Situation
1	Minimum component size
2	Cot bar width
3	Insulated handle

4 Why do pill bottles and bleach bottles need to have safety caps?

Dietary Needs

5 Circle the correct options in the following sentences.

a) An athlete will need a **higher / lower** energy or calorific intake than an office worker.

b) An elderly person will need a **higher / lower** energy intake than a 16-year-old boy.

6 Apart from energy requirement, give two other reasons why different people will eat different foods.

a)

b)

Consumer Protection

Regulations and Legislation

1 Choose the correct words from the options given to complete the following sentences.

voluntary **retailers** **regulations** **Acts of Parliament** **consumer** **compulsory**

When designing products you should be aware that there is a wide range of .... and legislations that are aimed at protecting the .... Some regulatory bodies are set up by manufacturing groups to ensure that all their members follow their .... codes of practice. Some regulations are governed by ....

2 Circle the correct options in the following sentences.

a) The **Food Safety / Sale of Goods** Act states that products must be fit for their purpose.

b) The **Food Safety / Sale of Goods** Act provides guidance on food hygiene management.

3 The table contains the names of five forms of legislation. Match descriptions **A, B, C, D** and **E** with the legislations listed **1–5** in the table. Enter the appropriate number in the boxes provided.

A Makes it illegal to sell products that are underweight or short-measured ☐

B Allows the Government to ban the sale of dangerous products ☐

C Makes it illegal to make false claims about a product ☐

D Prevents the sale of harmful or defective products ☐

E States that certain information must be included on labels ☐

	Legislation
1	Trade Descriptions Act
2	Consumer Protection Act
3	Weights and Measures Act
4	Consumer Safety Act
5	Food Labelling Regulations

Standards and Consumers' Association

4 What is a Kitemark? Tick the correct option.

A A test against nationally recognised standards ☐

B A test against locally recognised standards ☐

C A test of a product's strength ☐

D A test of a product's durability ☐

5 Explain what kind of information the *Which?* magazine publishes.

....

Branding

Brand Creation

1 Circle the correct options in the following sentences.

a) **Advertising / Branding** is about promoting a company's strengths.

b) **Advertising / Branding** is about promoting products in different target markets.

2 Which of the following statements describe valid promises that a business makes to its customers? Tick the **three** correct options.

A Giving best value for money in the marketplace ☐

B Offering the latest technology ☐

C Making a fast profit for the shareholders ☐

D Offering high-quality customer care ☐

Maintaining and Communicating the Brand

3 How can a company maintain its brand? Tick the **two** correct options.

A By producing products of a consistent quality ☐

B By not delivering products that it has promised it can ☐

C By producing products cheaply but to a very poor quality ☐

D By being honest about their product and what they can produce ☐

Protecting the Brand

4 What is intellectual property?

....

....

5 The table contains the names of four methods of brand protection.

Match descriptions **A**, **B**, **C** and **D** with the methods **1–4** in the table. Enter the appropriate number in the boxes provided.

	Brand Protection
1	Registered designs
2	Trademarks
3	Copyright
4	Patents

A Commonly used for protecting publications and building plans ☐

B Registered and protects names, symbols and logos ☐

C Offers proof of ownership and used to protect the form or style of a product or logo ☐

D Used to protect inventions, new technologies or new processes ☐

Branding

License Agreement

1. What is a license agreement? Tick the correct option.

   A A contract between the owner of an idea and the customer ☐

   B A contract between the owner of an idea and the manufacturer ☐

   C A contract between the manufacturer of an idea and the customer ☐

   D A contract between different manufacturers ☐

2. Choose the correct words from the options given to complete the following sentences.

   cartoon **image** **legal** **pictures** **brand** **license**

   The Disney corporation allow products to be manufactured that use their .... characters, but they have strict .... agreements that protect the .... and maintain the quality associated with Disney products. This is an essential part of maintaining their ....

Fairtrade Brand

3. **a)** What is the following logo?

   ....

   b) Explain what this logo means.

   ....

   ....

4. Which of the following statements describe the advantages to the producer of using the Fairtrade system? Tick the **two** correct options.

   A All the produce will be sold regardless of quality ☐

   B Producers can charge a high price for their goods ☐

   C An extra premium is invested in social or economic development projects ☐

   D A minimum price is paid that covers the cost of sustainable production ☐

Paper and Board

Paper

1 Choose the correct words from the options given to complete the following sentences.

wood **animal** **cellulose** **wood pulp** **vegetable** **mineral**

Paper is made from very fine .... fibres. The fibres are made of .... that is usually extracted from .... The raw material is known as ....

2 Number the following statements **1–4** to put them into the correct order to describe how paper is made. Put the appropriate number in the boxes provided.

A The pulp is then poured over a fine mesh. ☐

B The fibres are passed through rollers to remove the remaining excess water. ☐

C As the water drains away the cellulose fibres link together. ☐

D Chips of wood are cooked in water and chemicals to create a mushy wood pulp. ☐

3 What weight is paper normally measured in? ....

Board

4 Circle the correct options in the following sentences.

a) Paper and board can be given a full range of colours by adding **stains / dyes** to the pulp.

b) Very thick board is made by sticking sheets of paper or board together in a process known as **bonding / laminating**.

5 Over what weight is paper classed as board? Tick the correct option.

A 250g/m² ☐ **B** 200g/m² ☐ **C** 100g/m² ☐ **D** 150g/m² ☐

6 Match descriptions **A, B** and **C** with the materials **1–3** in the table. Enter the appropriate number in the boxes provided.

A Board for supporting paintings or posters ☐

B Board for making heavy-duty packaging ☐

C Containers for drinks / food ☐

	Material
1	Carton board
2	Mounting board
3	Corrugated board

7 What material can paper-based board be laminated with to make a composite material? Tick the correct option.

A Steel ☐ **B** Concrete ☐

C Plaster of Paris ☐ **D** Aluminium foil ☐

Types of Paper and Board

Types of Paper and Board

1 The table contains the names of three types of board.

Match descriptions **A**, **B** and **C** with the boards **1–3** in the table. Enter the appropriate number in the boxes provided.

A Can be laminated together to create thicker boards / general purpose material ☐

B Has insulating properties that can keep moisture in / out ☐

C Is cheap and strong, but not too heavy. ☐

	Board
1	Foil-lined board
2	Cardboard
3	Corrugated board

2 Complete the table.

Name	Description	Uses
Solid white board	A strong, high quality board that is very good for printing on. Made from pure bleached wood pulp.	**a)** ....
b)	A tough and lightly textured material that is often a very light cream colour. Takes coloured pencils well.	**c)** ....
Layout and tracing paper	**d)**	Used during the development stage of designing.
Duplex board	**e)**	Used on food packaging and is often only coated on one side for printing.

3 What weight does duplex board normally come in?

....

4 What weight does tracing paper normally come in?

....

Timber and its Natural Characteristics

Timber

1 Match descriptions **A**, **B** and **C** with the woods **1–3** in the table. Enter the appropriate number in the boxes provided.

A Timber sheets that are made by gluing together either wood layers or wood fibres ☐

B Come from slow-growing deciduous or broad-leafed trees ☐

C Come from fast-growing coniferous or needle-leafed trees ☐

	Wood
1	Hardwood
2	Softwood
3	Manufactured board

2 Which of the following properties is an advantage when using manufactured board? Tick the correct option.

A It has a beautiful grain ☐

B It's available in large sheets ☐

C It's much cheaper than solid wood ☐

D It's available in a variety of thicknesses ☐

3 Sketch a piece of plywood to show the way in which it is made.

4 Give a definition (description) for each of the following terms:

a) Grain pattern: ....

....

b) Workability: ....

....

c) Structural strength: ....

....

Hardwoods and Softwoods

Hardwoods and Softwoods

1 Describe, in as much detail as you can, the properties of beech.

2 Give three uses for ash.

a)

b)

c)

3 Describe, in as much detail as you can the properties of teak.

4 Match the uses **A**, **B**, **C** and **D** with the woods **1–4** in the table. Enter the appropriate number in the boxes provided.

	Wood
1	Ash
2	Mahogany
3	Teak
4	Beech

A An outdoor table

B A child's toy

C A hockey stick

D An indoor dining table

5 **a)** Why are thin layers of hardwood often glued onto manufactured boards such as MDF?

b) What is this technique called?

Manufactured Boards

1 What do the following acronyms stand for?

a) MDF ....

b) WBP ....

2 Circle the correct options in the following sentences.

a) Plywood / Chip board is a manufactured board made from waste materials.

b) Plywood / Chip board is a manufactured board made from veneers.

3 Give two uses for chip board.

a) ....

b) ....

4 Why is it necessary to cover the **edges** of manufactured boards? Tick the correct option.

A To make the product more expensive ☐

B To cover the lines or rough fibres ☐

C So varnish can be applied ☐

D To make the board stronger ☐

5 What kind of board is blockboard similar to? Tick the correct option.

A Hardboard ☐

B Chip board ☐

C MDF ☐

D Plywood ☐

6 Give two uses for blockboard.

a) ....

b) ....

Metals

Metals and their Properties

1 Circle the correct options in the following sentences.

a) Metals that contain mixtures of elements are said to be **non-ferrous / alloys / ferrous**.

b) Metals that don't contain any iron are said to be **non-ferrous / alloys / ferrous**.

c) Metals that contain iron are said to be **non-ferrous / alloys / ferrous**.

2 Give the two main properties of ferrous metals.

a) ....

b) ....

3 Name a common alloy.

....

Properties and Size of Metals

4 Match descriptions **A**, **B**, **C**, **D**, **E** and **F** with the properties **1–6** in the table. Enter the appropriate number in the boxes provided.

A The ability to accept bending or distorting ☐

B The ability to regain its original shape after it has been deformed ☐

C Resistance to scratching, cutting, denting and wear ☐

D The ability to be easily pressed, spread and hammered into shapes ☐

E Withstanding force without breaking or bending permanently ☐

F When the structure of the metal changes as a result of repeated hammering or strain ☐

	Material Property
1	Hardness
2	Work hardening
3	Flexibility
4	Strength
5	Elasticity
6	Malleability

5 What kind of sections do metals usually come in? Tick the **two** correct options.

A Curved bar ☐ **B** Round bar ☐

C Star section tube ☐ **D** Square tube ☐

6 Circle the correct options in the following sentence.

Metal sheets are usually sold in **metric / imperial** lengths and in **metric / imperial** thicknesses. ☐

Ferrous Metals

1 Complete the table below.

Metal	Description	Uses
a)	An alloy of iron with typically 18% chromium and 8% nickel. Very resistant to wear and corrosion and doesn't rust	**b)** ....
Mild steel	**c)**	Nuts and bolts, furniture frames, gates, girders
d)	Also known as 'medium' or 'high carbon' steel. Up to 1.5% carbon content. Strong and very hard	Hand tools, e.g. chisels, screwdrivers, hammers, saws, garden tools, springs
e)	Re-melted pig iron with some small quantities of other metals. 93% iron with 4% carbon is typical. Very strong in compression, but brittle	**f)** ....
High speed steel	Contains a high content of tungsten, chromium and vanadium. Brittle, but resistant to wear	**g)** ....

2 Match the uses **A**, **B**, **C** and **D** with the ferrous metals **1–4** in the table. Enter the appropriate number in the boxes provided.

A An outdoor table ☐ **B** A drill bit ☐

C A car brake drum ☐ **D** A car body ☐

	Ferrous Metal
1	Cast iron
2	Stainless steel
3	Mild steel
4	High speed steel

3 Which of the following properties would a designer be looking for if they chose stainless steel for a cutlery project? Tick the **two** correct options.

A It will look good when painted ☐ **B** It has an interesting yellow / gold colour ☐

C It's much cheaper than mild steel ☐ **D** It's unlikely to rust or corrode ☐

E It doesn't taste or taint the food ☐

4 Why is mild steel often painted?

....

Non-ferrous Metals and Alloys

Non-ferrous Metals and Alloys

1 Complete the table below.

Metal	Description	Uses
a)	Light grey in colour. Lightweight and anodised to protect the surface and to colour it	**b)** ....
Lead	**c)**	Car battery cells, weather proofing, plumber's solder
d)	Bright silver, ductile and malleable, resistant to corrosion	Coating on food cans
Copper	**e)**	**f)** ....

2 Match the properties **A**, **B** and **C** with the metals **1–3** in the table. Enter the appropriate number in the boxes provided.

A Very ductile, malleable and not affected by oxidation ☐

B Very weak and extremely resistant to corrosion ☐

C Very ductile and malleable, but does tarnish ☐

	Metal
1	Zinc
2	Gold
3	Silver

3 Which of the following properties would a designer be looking for if they chose copper for a project? Tick the **three** correct options.

A It has a beautiful deep red-brown colour ☐

B It's easy to work and is malleable ☐

C It's much cheaper than steel ☐

D It's unlikely to tarnish ☐

E It's easy to solder ☐

4 Circle the correct options in the following sentences.

a) **Brass / Casting alloy** is an alloy of copper and zinc.

b) **Brass / Casting alloy** is an alloy of aluminium, copper and silicon.

Thermosetting Plastics

Polymerisation

1 Choose the correct words from the options given to complete the following sentences.

polymerisation **properties** **links** **least** **monomers** **polymers** **chains**

There are many different plastics and they all have different .... Synthetic plastics are manufactured using a process known as .... This occurs when .... join together to form long .... of molecules called polymers.

2 What kind of plastic are amber and latex? Tick the correct option.

A Synthetic ☐ **B** Natural ☐ **C** Man-made ☐ **D** Thermoplastic ☐

Thermosetting Plastics

3 Fill in the table below.

Plastic	Description	Uses
Phenol formaldehyde	Hard, brittle plastic. Dark colour with a glossy finish. Heat resistant	**a)** ....
b)	**c)**	Laminated to form glass reinforced plastic
d)	Heat-resistant polymer	Tableware, electrical installations, decorative laminates and worktops

4 Circle the correct options in the following sentences.

a) **Bakelite / GRP / Urea formaldehyde** is a thermosetting composite plastic used to make car bodies and boats.

b) **Bakelite / GRP / Urea formaldehyde** is a thermosetting plastic used to make kettles, irons and saucepan handles.

c) **Bakelite / GRP / Urea formaldehyde** is a thermosetting plastic used to make electrical switches and electrical fittings.

Thermoplastics

Thermoplastics

1. What do the following acronyms stand for?

   a) HDPE ....

   b) HIPS ....

   c) PVC ....

2. Fill in the table below.

Plastic	Description	Uses
Polythene (high density)	a)	Pipes, bowls, milk crates and buckets
Perspex (Acrylic)	b)	Display signs, baths, roof lights and machine guards
c)	Light but strong plastic. Widely available in sheet form. Softens at about 95°C	Vacuum forming outer casings on electronic products, packaging
PVC	Stiff, hard-wearing. A plasticiser can be added to create a softer, more rubbery material	d) ....

3. What is low-density polythene used for? Tick the **two** correct options.

   A Milk crates ☐

   B Carrier bags ☐

   C Windows ☐

   D 'Squeezy' detergent bottles ☐

4. What property of PET makes it suitable to use for drinks bottles? Tick the correct option.

   A It's a coloured plastic ☐

   B It's transparent ☐

   C It's very rigid ☐

   D It's very brittle ☐

Clay and Ceramics

1 Circle the correct options in the following sentences.

Clay in moist form is called **body clay / slip.** Liquid clay used for decoration is known as **body clay / slip**.

2 What are ceramic materials? Tick the correct option.

- **A** Metallic, inorganic compounds ☐
- **B** Metallic, organic compounds ☐
- **C** Non-metallic, inorganic compounds ☐
- **D** Metals that have been processed ☐

3 Which of the following is **not** a ceramic product? Tick the correct option.

- **A** Tiles ☐
- **B** Sandstone ☐
- **C** Earthenware ☐
- **D** Bricks ☐

4 Why would it be advantageous to reinforce cement with steel rods?

....

5 What do the letters **GRP** stand for? ....

Engineering Ceramics

6 Circle the correct options in the following sentences.

a) Ceramic products formed from alumina and silicon nitride can be used for **computer disks / structural applications**.

b) Iron oxide particles are the active component in a variety of **computer disks / structural applications**.

7 What applications can ceramics be used in? Tick the **two** correct options.

- **A** Book shelves ☐
- **B** Car wheels ☐
- **C** Spark plugs ☐
- **D** Light bulbs ☐

Ceramic Materials

Ceramic Materials

1 Complete the table.

Ceramic	Description	Uses
a)	A white powder mixed with water to form a hard, white stone-like material that is soft enough to carve	b) ....
Glass	c)	Bottles and jars, windows, mirrors and cathode ray tubes. Glass fibres are used in GRP and as an insulation material in buildings
d)	Cheap and available worldwide. Fired at 900–1150°C. Porous, but need to be glazed.	e) ....

2 What is slip casting?

....

3 Match descriptions **A**, **B** and **C** with the ceramics **1–3** in the table. Enter the appropriate number in the boxes provided.

A Initially a pale grey colour and is fired at 1200–1280°C ☐

B White china clay mix that is fired at 1250–1300°C ☐

C One of the components of concrete ☐

	Ceramic
1	Porcelain
2	Cement
3	Stoneware clay

4 What are the components of mortar?

....

5 Match the uses **A**, **B** and **C** with the ceramics **1–3** in the table. Enter the appropriate number in the boxes provided.

A Bottles and windows jars ☐

B General tableware ☐

C Fine crockery 'China' ☐

	Ceramic
1	Porcelain
2	Glass
3	Stoneware clay

Fibres

1 What is a fibre? ....

2 Circle the correct options in the following sentences.

a) **Synthetic / Natural / Regenerated** fibres come from animals and plants.

b) **Synthetic / Natural / Regenerated** fibres come from natural, non-fibrous sources treated with chemicals.

c) **Synthetic / Natural / Regenerated** fibres are made from chemicals.

Yarns and Fabrics

3 The following stages describe how to spin yarn. Number them **1–3** to put them into the correct order. Enter the appropriate number in the boxes provided.

A Drawn into a sliver ready for spinning. ☐

B Carded to untangle the fibres to get them all the same way round. ☐

C Cleaned to remove dirt and waste. ☐

4 Choose the correct words from the options given to complete the following sentences.

threads **fibres** **ply** **clockwise** **anticlockwise** **bending** **distortion**

Yarn is made by spinning or twisting .... together. It's supplied by weight and .... The yarn is spun by twisting it .... (S twist) or .... (Z twist). More complex yarns are made by combining S twist and Z twist in equal amounts to prevent ....

5 Are the following statements **true** or **false**?

a) Fabric made into large sheets from yarn is called a **non-woven** material. ....

b) Felt is usually made by bonding loose fibres together. ....

6 In what measurements are fabrics sold / supplied? Tick the **two** correct options.

A Sold by the metric length ☐ **B** Supplied in standard widths, usually metric sizes ☐

C Sold by the imperial length ☐ **D** Supplied in standard widths, usually imperial sizes ☐

Natural and Regenerated Fibres

Natural and Regenerated Fibres

1 Complete the table below.

Fibre	Description	Uses
a)	b)	Knitted fabrics, sweaters, suits, dresses and carpets. Felt, flannel and gabardine
Silk	c)	Chiffon, organza, crepe and velvet. Dresses, shirts, ties
d)	A strong, absorbent, natural vegetable or cellulose fibre that comes from the cotton plant.	e) ....
Viscose	f)	Lingerie and underwear

2 Circle the correct options in the following sentences.

a) Linen is a natural vegetable fibre made from **cellulose / the stalks of the flax plant**.

b) Acetate is a regenerated fibre made from **cellulose / the stalks of the flax plant**.

3 Choose the correct words from the options given to complete the following sentences.

rigid **flexible** **wood pulp** **animal hair**

Regenerated fibres can be made from .... They have very .... properties and can be used as fibres for weaving.

4 From what material can viscose be made? Tick the correct option.

- **A** Wood pulp from a eucalyptus tree ☐
- **B** Wood pulp from an oak tree ☐
- **C** A plant stalk ☐
- **D** Fibres from a seed pod ☐

Synthetic Fibres

1 Complete the table below.

Fibre	Description	Uses
a)	A very soft and warm fibre similar to wool	b) ....
Polyamide (Nylon)	c)	Socks, tights and stockings. Upholstery, decorative furnishings, carpets. Lightweight sportswear
d)	e)	Cotton and polyester terry towels

2 Why would a polyester fabric be a good choice for the manufacture of sportswear? Tick the correct option.

A It's chemically produced from oil ☐
B It's easy to die bright colours ☐
C It creases easily ☐
D It's a lightweight fabric that is quick drying ☐

3 **a)** What is the common name for Elastane? Tick the correct option.

A Nylon ☐
B Acrylic ☐
C Wool ☐
D Lycra ☐

b) What properties of Elastane makes it a good choice to use for swimwear and sports clothing? Tick the correct option.

A It's very soft ☐
B It's strong and very elastic ☐
C It's shrinks when washed ☐
D It's strong and very tough ☐

Food Materials

Food Groups

1 Match descriptions **A, B, C, D** and **E** with the food groups **1–5** in the table. Enter the appropriate number in the boxes provided.

- **A** Needed to help in building the body and controlling how it works ☐
- **B** Needed for body growth and repair ☐
- **C** Needed for energy and to keep the body healthy ☐
- **D** Needed to provide energy and work with proteins to aid growth and repair ☐
- **E** Needed to prevent illness and control the release of energy in the body ☐

	Food Group
1	Carbohydrates
2	Minerals
3	Fats
4	Proteins
5	Vitamins

Healthy Eating

2 The Government has produced guidelines to help people maintain a balanced diet. Which of the following statements describe how a balanced diet can be achieved? Tick the **three** correct options.

- **A** Eat plenty of foods rich in starch and fibre ☐
- **B** Don't eat too many fatty or sugary foods ☐
- **C** Only eat fruit ☐
- **D** Eat a variety of different foods ☐
- **E** Boil all vegetables for at least 1 hour ☐

3 What is the 'five a day' campaign aimed at getting everyone to eat five portions of? Tick the correct option.

- **A** Sugar ☐
- **B** Meat ☐
- **C** Cheese ☐
- **D** Fruit and vegetables ☐

4 Circle the correct words in the following sentences.

You should think about the **nutritional / calorific** value of the food materials used in manufacturing food products. **High / Low** fat food products are now often available. You need to make sure that you eat the right amount to be a healthy **weight / height** for your **weight / height**.

Food Groups

1 Complete the table below.

Food	Description	Tips	Ideal Proportion of Diet
a)	**b)**	Eat fresh fruits and vegetables as some vitamins are lost during processing	Large proportion
c)	Provide starchy carbohydrates and fibre that are a good source of energy	**d)**	Large proportion
Meat, fish, nuts, beans, pulses and other proteins	**e)**	Grill food and trim excess fat from meat	**f)** ....
Milk and dairy products, e.g. cheese and yoghurt	**g)**	**h)**	Moderate proportion

2 Circle the correct option in the following sentence.

Vegetable-based foods are naturally **high / low** in fat.

3 **a)** Why should fatty and sugary foods make up only a small proportion of a healthy diet?

....

b) Name three fatty foods.

i) .... **ii)** .... **iii)** ....

c) Name three sugary foods.

i) .... **ii)** .... **iii)** ....

4 Suggest one tip for cutting down on unhealthy foods.

....

Properties of Food Materials

Properties of Food Materials

1 Match descriptions **A**, **B**, **C** and **D** with the processes **1–4** in the table. Enter the appropriate number in the boxes provided.

A Food set using eggs and starches ☐

B Food made crumbly by using fat ☐

C Food stuck together using eggs, milk or water ☐

D Food that is given a light texture by whipping ☐

	Process
1	Aeration
2	Thickening
3	Shortening
4	Binding

2 Circle the correct options in the following sentences.

When sugar is heated it becomes liquid and turns brown. This is known as **caramelisation / aroma**. Herbs, spices, sugar, fruit and vegetables can improve the **caramelisation / aroma** of food.

3 What kind of flavour do chillies create? Tick the correct option.

A Smooth ☐

B Hot ☐

C Sweet ☐

D Sickly ☐

4 Choose the correct words from the options given to complete the following sentences.

white **mayonnaise** **emulsifier** **sweets** **yolk** **margarine**

An .... stops fat or oil separating from a mixture. Egg .... is often used. Egg is added to salad dressings such as .... Emulsifiers are used in cakes, chocolate and ....

5 What materials can be used to hold burgers together until they are cooked?

....

6 Circle the correct options in the following sentences.

a) Egg **thickens / coagulates** when it's cooked and can be used to set a quiche.

b) Starch **thickens / coagulates** when it's heated and can be used to make sauces and custards.

☐

Standard Components

1 Choose the correct words from the options given to complete the following sentences.

cheap **products** **expensive** **specialist** **mass-produced** **slowly** **quickly** **quality**

Pre-manufactured standard components can be found in many .... and industries.

These components are .... by .... manufacturers so they're

.... to buy and products can be made .... and are easy to

assemble. The consistency and .... of products can also be maintained.

2 What is a disadvantage to producers when using pre-manufactured standard components?

....

Textile and Food Industry Components

3 What are valid reasons for textile manufacturers to use standard components? Tick the **two** correct options.

- **A** The product will look better
- **B** To fasten and unfasten parts of the product securely
- **C** As a decorative feature
- **D** To appeal to the teenage market

4 Which of the following would food industry manufacturers use as standard components? Tick the **three** correct options.

- **A** Ready-made sauces
- **B** Unwashed potatoes
- **C** Ready-made pastry
- **D** Herbs and spices

5 Which of the following would food industry manufacturers use as part-made components? Tick the **two** correct options.

- **A** Ready-made sauces
- **B** Pizza bases
- **C** Icing decorations
- **D** Washed and prepared vegetables

Vehicle and Furniture Components

6 Which of the following would the car manufacturing industry **not** use as standard components? Tick the correct option.

- **A** Steel sheet
- **B** Seatbelts
- **C** Nuts and bolts
- **D** Fan belts

Components

Vehicle and Furniture Components (Cont.)

1 Which of the following would the car manufacturing industry be able to use for different makes and models of car? Tick the **two** correct options.

A Batteries ☐ **B** Body shells ☐ **C** Tyres ☐ **D** Engine blocks ☐

2 Which of the following components would the furniture industry be able to use for different types of furniture? Tick the **two** correct options.

A Screws ☐ **B** Table tops ☐ **C** Pine planks ☐ **D** Hinges ☐

Control Components

3 Explain how electronic and mechanical components are important in the control of a car.

....

....

Systems

4 Choose the correct words from the options given to label the four boxes shown.

output **feedback** **input** **manufacturing** **process** **decision**

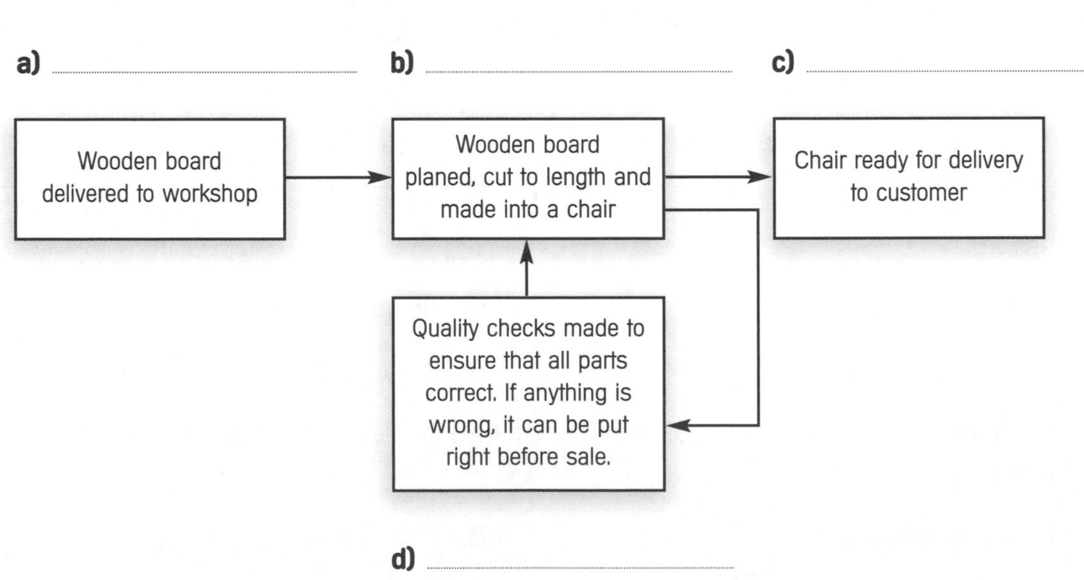

a) ....
b) ....
c) ....
Wooden board delivered to workshop
Wooden board planed, cut to length and made into a chair
Chair ready for delivery to customer
Quality checks made to ensure that all parts correct. If anything is wrong, it can be put right before sale.
d) ....

5 Give an example of where an electronic system controls a mechanical system.

....

6 Give an example of where a mechanical system controls an electronic system.

....

Electronics and Mechanisms

1. What can the functions of individual components be replaced by? Tick the correct option.

   A Integrated controls ☐ B Integrated electronics ☐
   C Integrated circuits ☐ D Integrated systems ☐

2. What kind of chip can be programmed? ....

3. a) What type of movement is shown by the arrow below? Tick the correct option.

   A Linear ☐
   B Reciprocating ☐
   C Rotary ☐
   D Oscillating ☐

   b) Give one example of such a movement.

   ....

4. a) What type of movement is shown by the arrow below? Tick the correct option.

   A Linear ☐
   B Reciprocating ☐
   C Rotary ☐
   D Oscillating ☐

   b) Give one example of such a movement.

5. Give one example of reciprocating movement.

   ....

6. Choose the correct words from the options given to complete the following sentences.

   movement **easier** **quicker** **input force** **output force** **angles**

   Mechanisms are designed to make tasks .... to carry out. They generate a force and .... in a product. When deciding on a particular mechanism to use, you need to look at the .... and movement available, and .... and movement required.

Electronic Components

Electronic Components

1 Match descriptions **A**, **B** and **C** with the components **1–3** in the table. Enter the appropriate number in the boxes provided.

A Can be used to amplify current ☐

B Provides the energy to the circuit ☐

C Controls input in most circuits ☐

	Component
1	
2	
3	

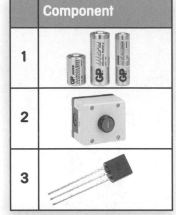

2 Complete the table below.

Electronic Component	Description	Uses
Resistors	**a)**	Used with capacitors to control the time it takes to charge the capacitor. Variable resistors can alter the sensitivity of a circuit
b)	Store electrical charge. When 'charged up' there is a voltage across the two leads	**c)** ....
d)	**e)**	Created for specific tasks, e.g. timing (the 555 timer is a common IC)

3 What kind of different switches are there? Tick the **two** correct options.

A Push to make ☐ **B** Toggle ☐

C Break to push ☐ **D** Jiggle ☐

4 Why are PIC chips different from IC chips? Tick the correct option.

A PIC chips can't be programmed ☐ **B** PIC chips can be clipped into place ☐

C PIC chips can made very cheaply ☐ **D** PIC chips can be programmed ☐

5 What are integrated circuits (ICs) often known as? Tick the correct option.

A Silicon chips ☐ **B** Fission chips ☐

C Timer chips ☐ **D** Electric chips ☐

Output Devices

1. What do the following letters stand for?

   a) DC .... **b)** DPDT ....

2. Complete the table below.

Output Device	Description	Uses
a)	Convert electrical energy into rotational movement	**b)** ....
Buzzers	**c)**	Warning devices, e.g. alarm circuits
d)	**e)**	Torches and lights on children's toys
Loudspeakers	**f)**	**g)** ....

3. How can the direction of rotation be changed electrically on a DC motor? Tick the correct option.

   A By changing over the connections to the battery ☐
   B By changing over the wires in the mains ☐
   C By using a different motor ☐
   D By using gears to reverse the direction ☐

4. What can a designer do to save energy when designing a circuit for a small torch? Tick the **two** correct options.

   A Use mains electricity ☐ **B** Use solar panels to re-charge batteries ☐
   C Use disposable batteries ☐ **D** Use a wind-up clockwork system ☐

5. Why might a designer use rechargeable batteries?

....

☐

Mechanical Components

Mechanical Components

1 Circle the correct option in the following sentence.

Cams are relatively simple devices that convert **oscillating motion to linear motion / rotary motion to reciprocating motion.**

2 The diagram shows a cam mechanism.

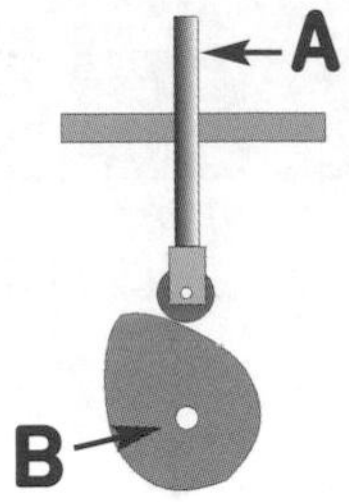

a) What is part A called? Tick the correct option.

A Follower ☐ **B** Guide ☐

C Cam ☐ **D** Crank ☐

b) What is part B called? Tick the correct option.

A Follower ☐ **B** Guide ☐ **C** Cam ☐ **D** Crank ☐

3 Where would you find a crank mechanism? Tick the correct option.

A In the pedal mechanism of a tricycle ☐

B A car steering system ☐

C A car engine camshaft ☐

D A toy that makes a noise as the wheels rotate ☐

4 Where would you find a rack and pinion mechanism? Tick the correct option.

A In the pedal mechanism of a tricycle ☐ **B** A car engine valve opening system ☐

C A car engine crankshaft ☐ **D** A car steering system ☐

5 Circle the correct options in the following sentences.

Gears are linkages for transferring **speed / motion**. Gear wheels have **teeth / sprockets** around the edge, which **stick / mesh** with the teeth of another gear. Gear systems may also be **fastened / linked** to chains or belts. Gears are used as **distance / speed** multipliers or reducers to make things go faster or slower.

6 Match descriptions **A**, **B** and **C** with the mechanisms **1–3** in the table. Enter the appropriate number in the boxes provided.

A The follower runs against the rotating cam and produces a reciprocating motion ☐

B Usually connected by belts ☐

C When driven by a piston this will produce a rotary motion ☐

	Mechanism
1	Pulley
2	Crank
3	Cam and follower

Mechanical Components (Cont.)

7 Complete the table below.

Mechanical Component	Name	Description and Use
	a)	Used together and in groups to change direction or speed. For example, gearboxes.
b)	Worm and worm wheel	c) ....
	d)	Changes motion through 90°. Gears of different sizes will create a change in speed. For example, electric hand drills.
e)	f)	Changes rotary motion into linear motion. For example, steep railway tracks.

8 The table contains the names of four gear systems that can be used for engineering.

Match descriptions **A**, **B**, **C** and **D** with the systems **1–4** in the table. Enter the appropriate number in the boxes provided.

A Used in cars to convert the rotary motion of the steering wheel into a lateral movement of the wheels ☐

B The small pinion moves the big pinion, which has twice as many teeth and so rotates at half the speed ☐

C Changes motion through 90° giving a large reduction in speed and a high torque ☐

D Changes motion through 90° and if the gears are different sizes there will be a change in speed as well ☐

	Gear System
1	Bevel gears
2	Pinions
3	Worm and worm wheel
4	Rack and pinion

Mechanical Components

Mechanical Components (Cont.)

9 Choose the correct words from the options given to complete the following sentences.

comfortable **pedals** **lubricated** **chain** **sprocket** **pinion** **stretch**

The chain on a bicycle connects the .... to the back wheel. As the pedal is pushed by your feet the .... links with the .... and the wheel turns. Different sized sprockets make it possible to pedal at a .... speed when there are hills. A chain doesn't .... or slip and has a direct drive, but it's difficult to change and has to be .... with oil.

10 What are the advantages of a pulley system? Tick the **two** correct options.

- **A** Gives a direct drive ☐
- **B** Doesn't slip ☐
- **C** Doesn't need to be lubricated ☐
- **D** Easy to change ☐

11 Circle the correct options in the following sentences.

A pulley is a wheel with a groove around it in which runs a **chain / belt.** A sprocket is a wheel with teeth around it on which runs a **chain / belt.**

12 What is the best way to reverse direction in a pulley system? Tick the correct option.

- **A** Run it more slowly ☐
- **B** Include a gear box in the system ☐
- **C** Put a twist in the belt ☐
- **D** Change the belt for a chain ☐

13 Match descriptions **A**, **B** and **C** with the mechanical components **1–3** in the table. Enter the appropriate number in the boxes provided.

- **A** Works in a similar way to a pulley and belt, but with less risk of slippage ☐
- **B** Transfers motion between mechanisms ☐
- **C** A rigid bar that pivots around a fulcrum ☐

	Mechanical Component
1	Levers
2	Linkages
3	Chain and sprocket

14 Circle the correct options in the following sentences.

a) Pneumatic cylinders give reciprocating motion using compressed **fluid / air**.

b) Hydraulic cylinders provide reciprocating motion using compressed **fluid / air**.

New Materials and Smart Materials

1 Choose the correct words from the options given to complete the following sentences.

properties **special** **smart** **output** **safety** **input**

The rapid advance in new materials offers exciting possibilities in a range of industries.

.... materials react and change their .... in response to an

...................................., for example electrical current, heat and light. They are very useful in health

and .... situations, e.g. to give warning of heat.

Polymers, Metal Clays and Composites

2 Match descriptions **A**, **B** and **C** with the new materials **1–3** in the table. Enter the appropriate number in the boxes provided.

A Incorporates electronics into textiles ☐

B Looks and is worked like clay, but when heated it becomes solid metal ☐

C Made from corn or potato starch ☐

	New Material
1	Starch-based polymers
2	Quantum tunnelling composites
3	Precious metal clay

3 What are valid reasons for using starch-based polymers? Tick the **two** correct options.

A They're biodegradable ☐ **B** They're very cheap to manufacture ☐

C They use up spare food ☐ **D** They don't give off toxic fumes when burned ☐

4 What percentage of real metal is found in a precious metal clay? Tick the correct option.

A 92% ☐ **B** 96.5% ☐ **C** 98% ☐ **D** 99.9% ☐

5 Briefly explain what a quantum tunnelling composite is. ....

....

Carbon Fibres and Foamed Metals

6 Circle the correct options in the following sentences.

Some metal can be processed so that it **expands / foams**. When it's **sandwiched / toasted** between two solid sheets it produces a material that is **heavier / lighter**, **more flexible / stiffer** and **more / less** resistant to impact than solid sheet metal.

☐

Smart Materials

Smart Textiles and Pigments

1 What happens to smart colours when they're heated? Tick the correct option.

A They glow in the dark ☐ B They change shape ☐

C They are radioactive ☐ D They change colour above 27°C ☐

2 Circle the correct option in the following sentence.

Smart colours are a range of **thermochromic / thermoplastic** pigments that react to changes in temperature.

3 What could a designer use smart colours for? Tick the **three** correct options.

A Temperature indicators on a kettle to indicate when it's boiling ☐

B Temperature indicators on mugs to indicate safe temperatures ☐

C Additions to jewellery ☐

D Wallpaper that can indicate room temperature ☐

Shape Memory Alloys and Nanotechnology

4 Choose the correct words from the options given to complete the following sentences.

bent **remember** **heated** **shape memory alloys** **returns** **cooled** **hit**

A smart alloy is a material that can .... its original shape, for example Nitinol wire. Other .... have a 'memory' of their original shape. When the alloy is .... or twisted, it keeps its new shape until it's .... When the temperature is raised to a certain level the alloy .... to its original shape.

5 What happens to Nitinol wire when a small electric current is passed through it? Tick the correct option.

A It will heat up ☐ B It will expand in length ☐

C It will change colour ☐ D It will shrink in length ☐

6 What can a nano material be used for? Tick the **two** correct options.

A Self-cleaning materials ☐

B Lubricants ☐

C In paint as a colour ☐

D In solid drugs to make them dissolve better ☐

☐

Manufacturing & Scales of Production

Primary and Secondary Processing

1 Circle the correct options in the following sentences.

a) **Secondary / Primary** processing turns raw materials into useful standard stock sizes.

b) **Secondary / Primary** processing turns standard stock materials into manufactured products.

2 Match descriptions **A**, **B**, **C**, **D**, **E** and **F** with the stages **1–6** in the table. Enter the appropriate number in the boxes provided.

A Changes both the size and the shape of the material ☐

B Changes the shape and size of the material, but doesn't change the volume ☐

C The surface finish of a material, normally achieved by applying some form of coating, e.g. paint ☐

D Joining materials together through bonding, e.g. welding and adhesives ☐

E Changes the internal properties of a material, e.g. making it stronger or more elastic ☐

F The pouring or forcing of liquid or non-solid material into moulds ☐

	Stages
1	Forming
2	Assembling
3	Finishing
4	Casting and moulding
5	Wastage
6	Conditioning

Scales of Production

3 Complete the table below.

Production System	Description	Example of Product
a)	Only one product is made at a time	b) ....
Batch	c)	d) ....
Continuous production	e)	f) ....

Scales of Production and Computer Technology

Scales of Production (Cont.)

1 Circle the correct options in the following sentences.

Batch / Just in time production involves the arrival of **broken / component** parts at exactly the time they are needed at the factory. Little storage space is required, which saves on warehousing **budgets / costs**. But, if the supply of components is stopped, the production line is **interrupted / speeded up**, which then becomes very costly.

2 What do mass production systems always make use of? Tick the **two** correct options.

- **A** 24/7 working
- **B** A production line where different workers are responsible for different jobs
- **C** Batches of thousands of the same product being made
- **D** Quality control

ICT and Remote Manufacturing

3 What kind of system has the improvements in ICT meant that different manufacturing functions can be combined into? Tick the correct option.

- **A** Partially operated systems
- **B** Fully automated systems
- **C** Partially automated systems
- **D** Systems solely operated by people

4 What does manufacturing **remotely** mean? Tick the correct option.

- **A** Design decisions can be made by remote control
- **B** No one takes responsibility for the consistency of manufacture
- **C** The designer and manufacturer are in different locations
- **D** The manufacturer is in a remote location where they are hard to contact

5 Give two communication methods that make it easy to keep in contact when manufacturing remotely.

a) ....

b) ....

Computer Technology and Production Systems

CAM, CNC and CAD

1 What do the following letters stand for?

a) CAM ....

b) CNC ....

c) CAD ....

2 What is post processing?

....

3 Why would a manufacturer choose to make their products on a computer controlled system? Tick the **two** correct options.

- **A** They are slow to make ☐
- **B** Receiving plans by email is easy ☐
- **C** The production will be very fast ☐
- **D** It's difficult to change size or shape ☐
- **E** Very accurate details can be cut ☐
- **F** Each piece will be slightly different ☐

Electronic Product Definition

4 Choose the correct words from the options given to complete the following sentences.

changes **difficulties** **processing** **information** **database**

Electronic product definition allows all product and .... data to be stored electronically in one large .... Everyone working on a project can then access the .... and everyone is kept aware of any .... / amendments.

Manufacturing

5 Give two systems or groups of systems that commercial manufacturing consists of.

a) ....

b) ....

Health, Safety and Risk Assessment

6 Give two examples of health and safety systems that it's important that you know / follow.

a) ....

b) ....

7 What is a **risk assessment**? ....

....

Quality Assurance Systems

Quality Assurance and Quality Control

1 Circle the correct options in the following sentences.

a) Methods built into the production system before and during manufacture are quality **control / assurance** issues.

b) Checks carried out during manufacture are quality **control / assurance** issues.

2 How can members of the public be involved in the monitoring of products? Tick the **two** correct options.

- **A** By complaining when something goes wrong ☐
- **B** By filling in questionnaires ☐
- **C** By being deliberately sold broken products so that they will return them ☐
- **D** By working in a factory for a day to see how difficult it is ☐

3 Choose the correct words from the options given to complete the following sentences.

testing **measuring** **thickness** **smell** **diameter** **taste** **screws**

Sampling is an important part of the .... of a manufactured product and can take place at any time during production. An injection-moulded plastic bottle top could be tested for .... and .... and to check whether it .... onto its container properly.

4 Which of the following are valid quality control checks? Tick the **two** correct options.

- **A** Price ☐
- **B** Taste ☐
- **C** Dimensional accuracy ☐
- **D** Popularity ☐

Tolerances

5 Why would you use an analysis of tolerance test? Tick the **two** correct options.

- **A** To get public feedback ☐
- **B** To help achieve zero faults ☐
- **C** To help achieve 10% faults ☐
- **D** To signal the imminent failure of a machine or a tool ☐

☐

Moulding Food

1 Circle the correct options in the following sentences.

The simplest form of **moulding / forging** is used for food products, e.g. chocolate, sweets and jellies. When making jelly, the fruit juice and gelatine mixture is **cooled / heated** and poured into an aluminium or plastic **sheet / mould**. Once **frozen / cool** the set jelly can be emptied from the mould.

2 How can moulds for jelly and chocolate be made in a school workshop? Tick the correct option.

A By vacuum forming plastic sheet

B By injection moulding

C By vacuum forming food-grade polystyrene

D By rotational moulding

Split Pattern Sand Casting

3 Number the following stages of the pattern casting process **1–8** to put them into the correct order.

A One of the boxes has two tapered wooden pegs or sprues.

B The space left is filled with molten metal.

C Oil-bound sand is used to fill each box.

D The pattern is made in two halves and attached to a board.

E The pattern is removed carefully.

F The pattern is sandwiched between open boxes called a cope and drag.

G The cope and drag are put back together.

H A pattern is made from a timber such as MDF or Jelutong.

4 Label each part of the diagram below.

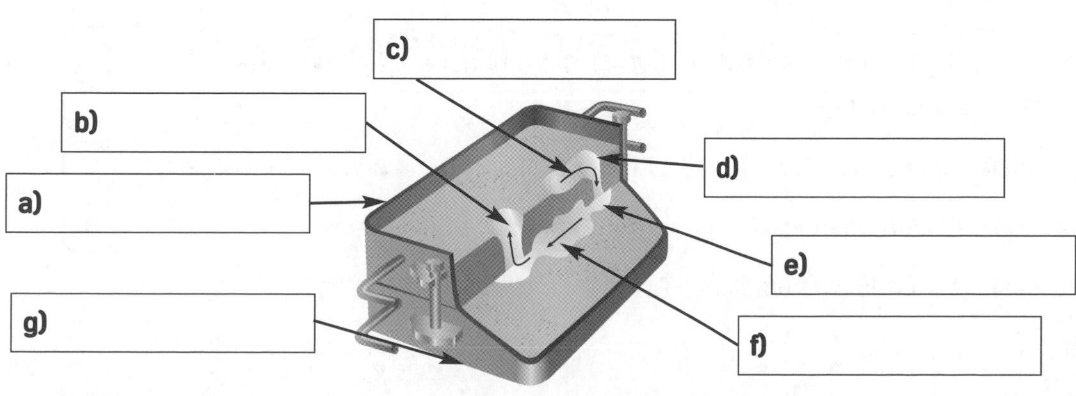

Casting

Lost Pattern Casting

1 Give an example of a metal that lost pattern casting is used to form.

2 Why is it important to wear a face mask when casting aluminium? Tick the **two** correct options.

- **A** Poisonous fumes are given off
- **B** Great heat is given off
- **C** Lots of sparks are given off
- **D** Lots of dust is given off

Die Casting

3 What kind of metal would you mould in a die-casting process? Tick the correct option.

- **A** Ferrous metal
- **B** Alloy
- **C** Non-ferrous metal
- **D** Copper

4 How is a die-cast mould cooled?

5 Which of the following statements describe how you can die cast in school? Tick the **two** correct options.

- **A** Using an oxy-acetylene torch
- **B** Using a sand casting box
- **C** Using pewter melted with an electric paint stripper gun or a blowlamp
- **D** Using a mould machined out of MDF or blocks of Necuron

Slip Casting

6 Number the following stages **1–6** to put them into the correct order.

- **A** Once dry the plaster mould can be re-used.
- **B** The slip is poured out and the casting is left to dry and harden.
- **C** The liquid clay (slip) is poured into the mould.
- **D** A plaster of Paris mould is made in two or more parts and held together with large rubber bands.
- **E** The plaster draws the moisture out of the slip and forms the wall of the casting.
- **F** The mould is then opened and the casting is removed.

7 What is slip casting used to manufacture? Tick the correct option.

- **A** Aluminium products
- **B** Timber products
- **C** Concrete products
- **D** Ceramic products

Moulding Plastics

Injection Moulding

1 Number the following processes **1–4** to put them into the correct order.

A Pressure is maintained on the mould, until it has cooled enough to be opened. ☐

B Plastic powder or granules are fed from the hopper into a hollow steel barrel. ☐

C Once enough melted plastic has collected, the hydraulic system forces the plastic into the mould. ☐

D The heaters melt the plastic as the screw moves it along towards the mould. ☐

2 What are the typical materials used in injection moulding? Tick the **two** correct options.

A Polythene and polystyrene ☐

B Expanded polystyrene and polyurethane ☐

C Melamine and urea formaldehyde ☐

D Polypropylene and nylon ☐

Blow Moulding

3 Circle the correct options in the following sentences.

Common materials used for blow moulding are PVC, **acrylic / polythene** and polypropylene. This process is similar to the **extrusion / vacuum** process, apart from the use of an **water / air** supply and a **halving / split** mould instead of the **cooling / heated** chamber.

4 Explain what a parison is. ....

....

Rotational Moulding

5 Number the following stages **1–5** to put them into the correct order.

A The mould splits apart to put plastic inside. ☐

B On cooling, the mould is opened up and the product is ejected. ☐

C Heat is applied while the mould is rotated. ☐

D The plastic is poured into the mould. ☐

E Plastic is thrown outwards to the inner surface of the mould. ☐

6 Give two products that can be made by rotational moulding.

a) .... **b)** ....

Forming

Drop Moulding / Drape Forming

1 Circle the correct options in the following sentences.

a) The process of laying clay inside a mould is called **drop moulding / drape forming**.

b) The process of laying clay outside a mould is called **drop moulding / drape forming**.

2 Which of the following materials could be used for producing a mould for forming pastry? Tick the **two** correct options.

A Ceramic ☐ **B** Glass ☐ **C** Plaster of Paris ☐ **D** Wood ☐

3 Which description best describes the drape moulding of plastic? Tick the correct option.

A A sheet of plastic is sucked into a mould and held until cool ☐

B A large force is used to squash a cube of polymer into a heated mould ☐

C A piece of plastic is moulded with a two-part former ☐

D A large force is used to compress glass fibres until they melt ☐

Felt Blocking

4 Choose the correct words from the options given to complete the following sentences.

steam **dry** **moist** **hats** **pinned** **shoes** **stretched**

Felt blocking is a process of forming .... felt, and is often used to make .... The damp felt, moistened with water or ...., is pulled over a wooden block. The felt is .... using hands or simple tools and .... onto the wooden block until dry.

5 How can large quantities of identical or complex forms be blocked? Tick the correct option.

A Hydraulic presses can be used to press the felt over aluminium blocks ☐

B They can be vacuum formed over aluminium blocks ☐

C They can be cast over aluminium blocks ☐

Vacuum Forming

6 Which would be the most suitable plastic to use for vacuum forming? Tick the correct option.

A Foamed PVC ☐ **B** Epoxy resin ☐

C High impact polystyrene ☐ **D** Nylon ☐

Extrusion and Bending

Extrusion

1 Circle the correct options in the following sentences.

To extrude plastic, the **sheets / granules** are fed into the **hopper / cooling chamber** by the rotating screw. Then they are heated and the softened plastic is forced through a **die / screw** in a **short / continuous** stream. This creates long tube or sectional extrusions. The extrusions are then passed through a **cooling / heated** chamber and cut to the required length.

2 What materials are typically used in extrusion? Tick the correct option.

A Polythene, PVC and nylon ☐ **B** Expanded polystyrene and polyurethane ☐

C Melamine and urea formaldehyde ☐ **D** Polypropylene and polyester ☐

Bending Plastics and Metals

3 What is the difference between scoring and creasing a piece of card?

....

4 **a)** Explain what happens when a piece of plastic is line bent.

....

....

b) What is used to make sure that a piece of plastic being line bent is held at the correct angle? Tick the correct option.

A A jig ☐ **B** A line bender ☐

C A vacuum mould ☐ **D** A shape ☐

c) What is used to make sure that the line bender wire is kept at the correct temperature? Tick the correct option.

A A thermocouple ☐ **B** A thermostat ☐

C A thermometer ☐ **D** A thermochrome ☐

5 Match descriptions **A**, **B** and **C** with the bending techniques **1–3** in the table. Enter the appropriate number in the boxes provided.

	Bending Technique
1	Bending machines
2	Scoring
3	Folding bars

A Holding sheet metal in a vice and bending it by hand using a mallet ☐

B Holding sheet metal in a machine and bending it by lifting a lever ☐

C Holding card on a table and bending it by half-cutting along one side ☐

Bending and Forging

Pressing

1 What are presses controlled by? Tick the correct option.

- **A** Hydraulic rams ☐
- **B** Hydraulic jacks ☐
- **C** Hydraulic pumps ☐
- **D** Hydraulic levers ☐

2 Name two products that can be made by pressing.

a) .... **b)** ....

Hand and Drop Forging

3 Choose the correct words from the options given to complete the following sentences.

softens **grain** **reformed** **stronger** **crystals** **forging** **hardens** **weaker**

Steel can be heated until it .... By applying a force from a hammer or a press the metal can be .... This process is known as .... Forged components are much .... than components that have been shaped by cutting because the .... of the metal hasn't been interrupted.

4 Circle the correct words in the following sentences.

a) Blacksmiths forge metals using a(n) **hearth / anvil** to withstand the hammer blows.

b) Blacksmiths forge metals using a(n) **hearth / anvil** to heat the iron or steel.

5 Briefly explain how a component is drop forged.

....

....

Compression Moulding

6 Which description best describes compression moulding? Tick the correct option.

- **A** A sheet of plastic is sucked into a mould and held until cool ☐
- **B** A large force is used to squash a cube of polymer into a heated mould ☐
- **C** A piece of plastic is moulded over a former ☐
- **D** A large force is used to compress glass fibres until they melt ☐

Shearing and Die Cutting

Shearing

1 Match the descriptions **A**, **B** and **C** with the processes **1–3** in the table. Enter the appropriate number in the boxes provided.

A Sheet metal is stamped cold using hydraulic rams, which create massive pressure ☐

B Sheet metal is usually cut with heavy duty scissors ☐

C Sheet metal can be shaped in several ways, e.g. by using folding bars ☐

	Processes
1	Shearing
2	Bending
3	Pressing

2 Match descriptions **A**, **B** and **C** with the shearing processes **1–3** in the table. Enter the appropriate number in the boxes provided.

A Cutting pieces of fabric using a shearing action ☐

B Cutting pieces of food using a shearing action ☐

C Cutting thin pieces of sheet metal using a shearing action ☐

	Processes
1	Scissors
2	Tinsnips
3	Food processors

Die Cutting

3 Choose the correct words from the options given to complete the following sentences.

plastic **rubber** **fabrics** **metal** **forme** **compressed** **release**

Die cutting is used to cut sheet materials like card, ... and leather. A layer of foam .... surrounds the blade and is .... during cutting; it's used to .... the material from between the blades. Press-knife cutting is known as .... cutting in the packaging industry.

Die Cutting in School

4 If you make simple die cutting tools in school, what would you use to hold the dies in place? Tick the correct option.

A Cardboard blocks ☐

B MDF blocks ☐

C Rubber blocks ☐

D Metal blocks ☐

Sawing and Chiselling

Hand Saws and Power Saws

1 Circle the correct options in the following sentences.

Sawing is one of the oldest methods of cutting materials. Teeth are **square / triangular** shaped so that they remove a small amount of material on the **forwards / backwards** stroke. The blade is **waved / twisted** to make a cut wider than the blade to reduce **friction / force**. As a general guide, **two / three / four** teeth should be on the material at any time. Metal cutting saws have small teeth on blades supported in a **frame / jig**.

2 Circle the correct options in the following sentences.

a) Hand saws work on the **forwards / backwards** stroke.

b) Coping saws work on the **forwards / backwards** stroke.

3 Match the uses **A, B, C** and **D** with the machine saws **1–4** in the table. Enter the appropriate number in the boxes provided.

A Used to cut out fine detail in decorative sheet wood / metalwork ☐

B Used to reduce large pieces of material to the right size for working ☐

C Used to shape small pieces of material ☐

D Used to reduce large pieces of metal to the right size for working ☐

	Saw
1	Circular saw
2	Band saw
3	Scroll saw
4	Powered hacksaw

Chiselling Wood

4 Match the uses **A, B** and **C** with the processes **1–3** in the table. Enter the appropriate number in the boxes provided.

A Cutting across a joint to clean out waste ☐

B Digging out waste from a mortise by cutting the fibres into short lengths ☐

C Pushing down onto a waste surface to shape the end of a piece of wood ☐

	Process
1	Vertical paring
2	Chopping
3	Horizontal paring

5 What kind of cutting action do wood chisels use? Tick the correct option.

A Square-shaped action ☐

B Prism-shaped action ☐

C Wedge-shaped action ☐

D Circular-shaped action ☐

Chiselling, Planing and Drilling

Chiselling Metals, and Planes

1 Which of the following types of steel are suitable for making cold chisels for cutting metals? Tick the **two** correct options.

A High carbon steel ☐ **B** Hardened steel ☐ **C** High speed steel ☐

D Stainless steel ☐ **E** Tempered steel ☐ **F** A steel alloy ☐

2 Circle the correct options in the following sentences.

Planing works when a **wedge / square** shaped cutting blade is used to **drill / shave** off thin layers of wood. It's important to plane **along / against** the grain. Special planes with a **shallow / steep** cutting angle allow planing across the end grain.

Drilling

3 Choose the correct names from the options given to state which drill has made each of the three holes. Enter the appropriate number in the boxes provided.

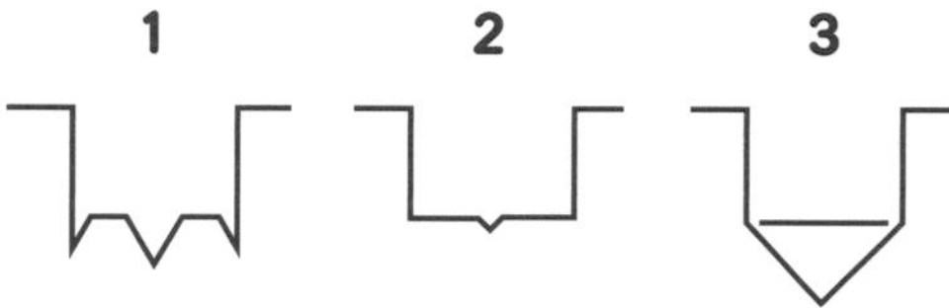

A Forstner bit ☐

B Twist bit ☐

C Auger bit ☐

4 Circle the correct options in the following sentences.

a) Drill bits are usually made from **high carbon / mild** steel.

b) Drill bits rotate **anti-clockwise / clockwise** when drilling.

5 What would a countersink bit be used for?

Power Drills and Pedestal Drills

6 Circle the correct options in the following sentences.

a) Mains powered drills are **safe / not safe** to use outside.

b) Battery powered drills are **safe / not safe** to use outside.

7 Circle the correct options in the following sentences.

Pedestal drills are also known as **pillar / portable** drills and can be bench or floor mounted. They provide a **safe / dangerous** and easy way of drilling materials. When drilling, the material must be firmly held in place by using a **vice / chuck** and the operator must wear **spectacles / goggles** or a visor.

Milling and Routing

Shaping Materials

1 Circle the correct options in the following sentences.

a) Shaping timber using a revolving, multi-toothed cutter is known as **milling / routing.**

b) Shaping metal or plastic using a revolving, multi-toothed cutter is known as **milling / routing.**

Routing and Milling

2 Which of the following statements describe a possible use for a hand-held router without jigs? Tick the correct option.

A Making round legs for a stool ☐ **B** Making a moulded edge around a table top ☐

C Cutting dovetail joints ☐ **D** Making a half-lap joint ☐

3 Choose the correct words from the options given to complete the following sentences.

CAD **manually** **CNC** **stepper motor** **CAM** **mechanically**

Traditional milling machines can be controlled by moving each axis .... By moving each axis with a ...., very accurate movements can be controlled using .... This is one of the most common forms of ....

4 Which of the following statements describe possible uses for CNC machining? Tick the **two** correct options.

A Manufacturing a knock-down kitchen ☐ **B** Manufacturing car parts ☐

C Carving a sculpture ☐ **D** Manufacturing baked beans ☐

5 Fill in the table to show the axis direction of a CNC milling machine.

Axis	Direction
a)	Left and right
b)	Front and back
c)	Up and down

Laser Cutting

6 Circle the correct options in the following sentences.

Lasers are now commonly used in schools to cut a variety of materials, including **fabrics / metals.** They are also used to **cut / engrave** hard plastics and glass. Laser cutters remove the **smallest / largest** amount of material and so are very accurate. **Air / Water** jet cutting is an alternative to laser cutting and is widely used in commercial production.

Metal-turning Lathe

1 Circle the correct option in the following sentence.

Turning metals and plastics on a centre lathe involves holding the work in a chuck and rotating the work **away from / towards** the cutter.

2 What is the tailstock used for? ....

....

Wood-turning Lathe

3 Name three different types of wood-turning chisel.

a) .... b) .... c) ....

4 Circle the correct options in the following sentences.

a) When using a wood-turning lathe, the tool is **rested on a support and is guided by hand / held in a tool post and guided by turning a wheel.**

b) When using a centre lathe, the tool is **rested on a support and is guided by hand / held in a tool post and guided by turning a wheel.**

5 In which ways can work be held securely when turning on a lathe? Tick the **two** correct options.

A The work can be held between centres ☐ **B** The work can be held by using a cramp ☐

C The work can be held in a machine vice ☐ **D** The work can be screwed onto a faceplate ☐

CNC Turning

6 What piece of machinery controls both the work and cutting tools on a CNC centre lathe? Tick the correct option.

A Hacksaw blade ☐ **B** Powered router ☐

C Stepper motor ☐ **D** Tank cutter ☐

7 What kind of items are CNC lathes generally used to turn? Tick the correct option.

A Large quantities of identical pieces ☐

B Small quantities of individual pieces ☐

C Large quantities of different shaped pieces ☐

D Small quantities of circular pieces ☐

Abrading

Abrasive Papers / Cloth

1 What materials are commonly used as abrasives for metal finishing? Tick the **two** correct options.

A Emery ▢ **B** Sand ▢ **C** Silicon carbide ▢ **D** Carborundum ▢

2 What materials are the abrasives for metal finishing glued onto? Tick the **two** correct options.

A Paper ▢ **B** Cardboard ▢ **C** Wood ▢ **D** Cloth ▢

3 What materials are commonly used as abrasives for wood finishing? Tick the **two** correct options.

A Glass ▢ **B** Sand ▢ **C** Garnet ▢ **D** Carborundum ▢

4 What kind of material is abrasive paper usually wrapped around? ....

Files

5 Circle the correct options in the following sentences.

Files are used to smooth and shape the surface of metals and hard plastics by **pushing / pressing** and **dragging / lifting** the hundreds of small **saws / teeth** on the file across the material.

Files are made from **mild / high carbon** steel and have been **softened / hardened** so they will cut other metals, even other **steel / glass**.

6 Draw a sketch of a three-square file.

Sanding Machines

7 What are sanding machines with abrasive discs that are designed for abrading woods called? Tick the correct option.

A Disc sanding machines ▢ **B** Emery machines ▢

C Linishers ▢ **D** Abraders ▢

8 What are sanding machines with a revolving belt of abrasive material that are designed for abrading metals called? Tick the correct option.

A Disc sanding machines ▢ **B** Emery machines ▢

C Linishers ▢ **D** Abraders ▢

Abrading and Cooking Food

Sanding Machines (Cont.)

1 What materials are commonly used as the abrasive material on sanding machines? Tick the correct option.

A Glass ☐ **B** Aluminium oxide ☐

C Garnet ☐ **D** Carborundum ☐

2 Suggest some safety precautions you should take when using powered sanding machines.

....

....

Cooking Methods

3 Which of the following statements does **not** describe a valid reason for cooking food? Tick the correct option.

A To tenderise, preserve or thicken ingredients ☐

B To preserve food for long periods ☐

C To bond ingredients together and change their structure ☐

D To change the taste of foods ☐

4 What kind of method of transferring heat does a cooker top use?

....

5 What kind of method of transferring heat does an oven use?

....

6 Circle the correct options in the following sentences.

Microwaves use **electrostatic / electromagnetic** waves that **vibrate / reflect** water molecules. This causes **frictional / thermal** heat.

Changes During Cooking

7 What structural changes happen when baking with yeast? Tick the **two** correct options.

A Holes formed by oxygen are left in the bread ☐

B The gluten sets which forms the bread structure ☐

C The yeast creates lots of carbon dioxide bubbles ☐

D The strands of carbon dioxide are tangled together ☐

Temperature Changes in Food

Storing and Keeping Food

1 Choose the correct words from the options given to complete the following sentences.

oxygen **bacteria** **pathogenic** **21°C** **warm** **cold** **121°C** **dormant**

If food isn't kept in the correct conditions, ... bacteria that cause food poisoning rapidly multiply. Bacteria thrive in ...., moist, non-acidic conditions containing plenty of .... Temperatures above .... destroy all bacteria and spores. Low temperatures slow down bacteria or make them .... but it doesn't kill them.

Chilling / Freezing Food

2 What does AFD stand for? ....

3 Match descriptions **A**, **B**, **C** and **D** with the chilling techniques **1–4** in the table. Enter the appropriate number in the boxes provided.

A Food is reduced from 0°C–18°C in 12 minutes ☐

B Food has been quick frozen then placed in a vacuum under reduced pressure ☐

C Food can be kept at 1°C–8°C for short-term storage ☐

D Food is rapidly cooled to 0°C–3°C in 90 minutes or less ☐

	Technique
1	Chilled
2	Cook-chilled
3	Quick freezing
4	AFD

Heating Food

4 Match descriptions **A**, **B** and **C** with the systems **1–3** in the table. Enter the appropriate number in the boxes provided.

A Liquid is heated and held at a high temperature for a short time then rapidly cooled ☐

B Food is heated to 110°C for 30 minutes ☐

C Food is heated to 120°C for 33 minutes before being cooled quickly and sealed in a container ☐

	System
1	Canning
2	Pasteurisation
3	Sterilisation

5 Circle the correct options in the following sentences.

Ultra heat-treatment (UHT) is when a **solid / liquid** is heated to a very high temperature for a **long / short** time. For example, milk is heated to **133°C / 93°C** for 1 second. This kills all the bacteria but doesn't affect the **shelf life / flavour**.

Heat Treatment of Materials

Annealing and Tempering

1 What is annealing? Tick the correct option.

- **A** Making a metal weak ☐
- **B** Making a metal very elastic ☐
- **C** Softening metal so it can be bent or hammered ☐
- **D** Hardening metal so it can be bent or hammered ☐

2 Why would you want to harden a piece of steel? Tick the correct option.

- **A** To make it very hard ☐
- **B** To make it very soft ☐
- **C** To make it workable ☐
- **D** To make it an attractive colour ☐

3 Circle the correct options in the following sentences.

a) Steel that will not wear away, but is brittle is said to be **tempered / hardened**.

b) Steel that is tough, but not brittle is said to be **tempered / hardened**.

4 Circle the correct options in the following sentences.

a) Ferrous metals are annealed by being heated to a cherry red (725°C) for a few minutes and then allowed to cool **quickly / slowly / very slowly.**

b) Copper is annealed by being heated to a dull red (500°C) and then allowed to cool **quickly / slowly / very slowly.**

Kiln Firing

5 Circle the correct options in the following sentences.

a) Biscuit firing (950°C–1000°C) **vitrifies / fuses** the clay.

b) Glaze firing (up to 1300°C) **vitrifies / fuses** the clay.

6 Explain what the term **firing** means.

....

7 Explain what the term **sintering** means.

....

Joining Timber

Joints

1 Choose the correct words from the options given to complete the joint chart below:

Joint	Description	Image
a)	Involves removing half the material from each piece to make a frame corner	b)
Dowel joint	c)	d)
e)	f)	

2 Match the uses **A**, **B**, **C** and **D** with the joints **1–4** in the table. Enter the appropriate number in the boxes provided.

	Joint
1	Housing joint
2	Dowel joint
3	Mitre joint
4	Lap joint

A Chair legs and cupboard corners ☐

B Strengthened with nails, and used in picture frame and carcase joints ☐

C Picture frames ☐

D Cupboard shelves ☐

3 What kind of joint is the strongest joint for box constructions? Tick the correct option.

A Mortise and tenon ☐ **B** Biscuit ☐

C Dovetail ☐ **D** Dowel ☐

Joining Timber

Screws and Nails

1 Name the three screw heads below.

a) b) c)

a) ....

b) ....

c) ....

2 Circle the correct options in the following sentences.

a) A **nail / screw** makes a very weak joint if used on its own.

b) A **nail / screw** can easily be removed and replaced in order to take things apart.

3 What are nailed joints correctly used for? Tick the **two** correct options.

A As a permanent fitting for chair legs ☐

B To hold wooden things together while the glue dries ☐

C As an axle for a toy car ☐

D To fit the backs of cupboards ☐

4 Why are cross head screws more popular than slot head screws? Tick the **two** correct options.

A They're easier to drive in using an electrically powered driver ☐

B They're very strong when used across the grain ☐

C They're useful for fixing other materials, such as metals or plastics, to timber ☐

D They're less likely to slip off the screwdriver ☐

Knock-down Fittings

5 Match the fastenings **A**, **B**, **C** and **D** with the joints **1–4** in the table. Enter the appropriate number in the boxes provided.

A A locking system, which has a cam that locks the parts together ☐

B A fitting that fits into a hole to provide a threaded insert that takes a machine screw ☐

C Plastic blocks used to take screws in each direction and are suitable for simple joints ☐

D A metal-screwed insert that sits in a hole and takes a machine screw ☐

	Joint
1	Cross dowel
2	Pronged nut
3	Modesty blocks
4	Cam bolt

Soldering and Welding

Joining Metals

1 Circle the correct options in the following sentences.

Metals can be joined permanently by welding where **ice / heat** is used to melt a pool of **the parent metals / a bonding metal.**

Soldering uses a **bonding alloy / filler rod** to form a joint.

Welding and Soldering

2 What does MIG stand for? ....

3 Describe what happens in MIG welding.

....

....

4 In what situation would you use gas welding?

....

5 What kind of metals are joined by TIG welding?

....

6 Circle the correct options in the following sentences.

a) When welding you must always wear **a dark visor / goggles** to protect your eyes.

b) When soft soldering you must always wear **a dark visor / goggles** to protect your eyes.

7 What is the difference between hard soldering and soft soldering?

....

....

8 Give a description of the following words.

a) Spelter: ....

b) Blowtorch: ....

Joining Metals and Plastics

Nuts, Bolts and Rivets

1 Match the joining methods **A**, **B**, **C** and **D** with the bolt / nut head types **1–4**. Enter the appropriate number in the boxes provided.

	Bolt / Nut Head Type	Picture
1	Hexagonal head	
2	Wing nut	
3	Slotted head	
4	Hexagonal socket head	

A Screwdriver ☐

B Allen key ☐

C Fingers ☐

D Spanner ☐

2 Choose the correct words from the options given to complete the following sentences.

nut **vibrating** **surface** **machine** **dismantled** **sprung** **used** **different** **protect**

Nuts and bolts can be .... for repair or maintenance. They also allow .... materials to be joined together. A washer is usually used under the .... to spread the pressure and .... the surface. This might be a plain ring or ...., which keeps the nut from .... loose.

3 Match the bolt heads **A**, **B** and **C** with the uses **1–3** in the table.
Enter the appropriate number in the boxes provided.

A Cheese head ☐

B Countersunk head ☐

C Hexagonal head ☐

	Uses
1	Will sit level with the surface
2	Tightened with a spanner
3	Best to be used on thin metals

4 What does the abbreviated description 'M12 x 25 Hex steel bolt' mean? ....

....

5 Circle the correct options in the following sentences.

a) A **pop / round head** rivet is the best method for riveting a tube onto a flat plate.

b) A **pop / round head** rivet is the best method for riveting two flat plates together.

Adhesives

Common School Adhesives

1 Match descriptions **A**, **B**, **C** and **D** with the adhesives **1–4** in the table. Enter the appropriate number in the boxes provided.

- **A** A waterproof adhesive, which is mixed into a creamy consistency with water ☐
- **B** A white, water-based adhesive ☐
- **C** A cheap and safe rubber solution ☐
- **D** Equal amounts of resin and hardener are mixed and set chemically to become very hard ☐

	Adhesive
1	Latex adhesive
2	PVA
3	Epoxy resin
4	Synthetic resin

2 What do the letters PVA stand for? ....

3 How does solvent cement work?

....

4 Which of the following adhesives would you use to glue a felt lining into a jewellery box? Tick the correct option.

- **A** Epoxy resin ☐
- **B** Synthetic resin ☐
- **C** Latex adhesive ☐
- **D** Hot melt glue ☐

5 Explain why you would **not** use a glue gun for a final outcome.

....

Industrial Adhesives

6 Which of the following is the common name for Cyanoacrylate? Tick the correct option.

- **A** Epoxy ☐
- **B** Superglue ☐
- **C** Latex ☐
- **D** Superstick ☐

7 Match descriptions **A**, **B** and **C** with the adhesives **1–3** in the table. Enter the appropriate number in the boxes provided.

- **A** Can be used instead of stitches in surgery ☐
- **B** Molecules in the material are vibrated under pressure and the heat generated creates an adhesive free-bond ☐
- **C** Expands and takes up space between poorly fitting parts ☐

	Adhesive
1	Polyurethane
2	Cyanoacrylate
3	Ultrasonic welding

Surface Finishes

Finishes

1 Why is a finish applied to wood? Tick the **four** correct options.

A To protect it from moisture ☐ **B** To protect it from insect attack ☐
C To make it less attractive ☐ **D** To enhance the colour of the grain ☐
E To make it easier to wipe the surface clean ☐ **F** To make it more expensive ☐

2 Why don't injection-moulded products need to be finished?

Paints

3 Which of the following types of finishes are suitable for giving wood surfaces a decorative *and* protective finish? Tick the **two** correct options.

A Gloss paint ☐ **B** Watercolour paint ☐
C Lacquer ☐ **D** Emulsion ☐

4 Which of the following statements are true for oil-based paints? Tick the **two** correct options.

A They are durable and suitable for both metals and timber ☐
B They dry more quickly than the other paint types ☐
C They are the most expensive type of paint to buy ☐
D They can be used internally or externally ☐

5 Which of the following statements is true for water-based paints? Tick the correct option.

A They are suitable for light use, e.g. on inside walls ☐
B They are durable and suitable for both metals and timber ☐
C They dry more quickly than the other paint types ☐
D They can be used internally or externally ☐

6 Which of the following statements are true for solvent-based paints? Tick the **two** correct options.

A They are the cheapest type of paint to buy ☐
B They are durable and suitable for both metals and timber ☐
C They dry more quickly than the other paint types ☐
D They can be used internally or externally ☐

Surface Finishes

Surface Finishes

1 The table contains the names of six types of finish. Match descriptions **A**, **B**, **C**, **D**, **E** and **F** with the finishes **1–6** in the table. Enter the appropriate number in the boxes provided.

	Finish
1	French polish
2	Cellulose
3	Wax polish
4	Polyurethane varnish
5	Wood stains
6	Sanding sealer

A Can be used to change the colour of the timber and show up the grain patterns

B Fills the porous surface of the timber and builds up a layer of polish on the material's surface

C A hard, quick-drying finish useful when wood turning

D A tough, heatproof and waterproof finish available in different colours with a matt, satin or gloss surface finish

E A solvent-based product similar to a varnish that is used to seal timber

F A quick-drying liquid that seals the surface and raises the fibres of the timber

2 Which of the following finishes are suitable for a piece of teak that is going to be used for a garden bench? Tick the correct option.

A No finish

B Wax polish

C Oil

D Silver polish

3 The table contains the names of four types of finish. Match the uses **A**, **B**, **C** and **D** with the finishes **1–4** in the table. Enter the appropriate number in the boxes provided.

	Finish
1	Oil
2	Gloss paint
3	Wood stain
4	French polish

A A metal window frame

B To colour a box before polishing

C An outdoor table

D An indoor dining table

Surfaces Finishes and Polishing

Plastic Dip-coating and Powder Coating

1 Circle the correct options in the following sentences.

Acrylic / Polythene is the most common **plastic / thermoplastic** powder that is used for plastic dip-coating. **Air / Water** is blown through the powder to make it behave like a **solid / liquid**. Metal, pre-heated to **180°C / 1000°C**, is dipped in the fluidised powder and returned to the **oven / mould** where it melts to form a smooth finish.

2 Which of the following products could be finished by plastic dip-coating? Tick the **two** correct options.

A Wooden tables ☐ **B** Dishwasher racks ☐

C Plastic tool handles ☐ **D** Steel coat hooks ☐

3 Which of the following statements are true about powder coating? Tick the **two** correct options.

A It provides a paint-like finish ☐ **B** It wears away quickly ☐

C It's available in all colours ☐ **D** It's not very durable ☐

Anodising, Plating and Galvanising

4 The table contains the names of three types of metal finishes. Match descriptions **A**, **B** and **C** with the finishes **1–3** in the table. Enter the appropriate number in the boxes provided.

	Finish
1	Plating
2	Anodising
3	Galvanising

A A process involving electrolysis that is used on aluminium to provide a durable finish ☐

B A thin layer of metal on the surface that provides a durable finish ☐

C A metal (usually mild steel) that is finished by being dipped into a bath of molten zinc ☐

Polishing

5 Why is polishing a very common finishing method used on timbers, metals and hard plastics? Tick the **two** correct options.

A Because it makes the surface waterproof ☐

B Because it makes the surface shine ☐

C Because it makes the surface a different colour ☐

D Because it makes the surface look better ☐

Polishing Materials

Polishing Timber

1 What kind of wax polish is normally used on timber? Tick the **two** correct options.

A Silicone wax ☐ **B** Candle wax ☐ **C** Beeswax ☐ **D** Petroleum wax ☐

2 Circle the correct options in the following sentences.

a) Wax is normally applied to wood using a **brush / cloth**.

b) Varnish is normally applied to wood using a **brush / cloth**.

Polishing Metals

3 Choose the correct words from the options given to complete the following sentences.

buffing **cutting** **abrasive** **liquid** **solid** **wax** **soft**

Metal polish is always slightly .... as it relies on cutting away the surface of the metal until it's very smooth. Metal polishes can be in .... form (applied with a cloth) or in a .... bar, which is applied to a .... wheel.

4 Which of the following metals is self-finished? Tick the correct option.

A Stainless steel ☐ **B** Steel ☐ **C** Copper ☐ **D** Silver ☐

Polishing Plastics

5 Why don't the surfaces of sheet plastics usually need to be finished unless they've been damaged?

....

6 Number the following stages of the plastic finishing process **1–4** to put them into the correct order.

A Different grades of wet and dry paper are wetted with water and used to make the edge smooth. ☐

B The edge is polished to a high shine using 'Brasso'. ☐

C A smooth file can be drawn along the edge of the plastic. ☐

D The edge is polished on a buffing wheel. ☐

7 What is the name for the finest type of filing that can be used on a plastic? Tick the correct option.

A Cross filing ☐ **B** Draw filing ☐

C Long filing ☐ **D** Short filing ☐

Glazing Ceramics

1. Choose the correct words from the options given to complete the following sentences.

glazed **glass** **chemicals** **coated** **flux** **melting** **seal**

Fired clay is .... in order to .... the surface. Clay is mixed with a .... and other .... which add colour and textures.

2. Which of the following materials are part of the mix that make up clay? Tick the **two** correct options.

A Alumina ☐ **B** Silica ☐ **C** Soil ☐ **D** Aggregate ☐

3. What is the usual temperature range for firing a glaze? Tick the correct option.

A 1220–1240°C ☐ **B** 1260–1280°C ☐
C 1240–1260°C ☐ **D** 1200–1220°C ☐

Glazing Food

4. The table contains the names of four types of food glazing.

Match descriptions **A**, **B**, **C** and **D** with the glazes **1–4** in the table. Enter the appropriate number in the boxes provided.

A Used to glaze ham ☐
B Used to glaze pastry ☐
C Used to glaze cakes ☐
D Used to glaze bread ☐

	Glaze
1	Beaten egg
2	Sugar syrup
3	Honey and orange mix
4	Milk

Enamelling

5. Choose the correct words from the options given to complete the following sentences.

glass **decorative** **1000°C** **melts** **1100°C** **sand** **evaporates**

During enamelling, a powdered .... mixture is evenly applied over the surface of the metal. The mixture is heated to .... and so ....

On cooling, a hard .... coating is formed on the metal.

Printing

Lithography

1 Explain what is meant by **offset lithography.** ....

....

2 What is a big advantage of using an offset method? Tick the correct option.

A It's quicker to make the plate ☐

B It's cheaper to make the plate ☐

C It's faster to print because it's a simple process ☐

D It's easier to check because the image is the right way round ☐

3 Circle the correct options in the following sentences.

In lithography, the unexposed parts of the plate **attract ink and reject water / reject ink and attract water** and the exposed parts of the plate **attract ink and reject water / reject ink and attract water**.

4 What are the specially treated plates for offset lithography printing normally made from? Tick the correct option.

A A steel sheet ☐ **B** Aluminium sheet ☐ **C** Thick board ☐ **D** Copper sheet ☐

5 How many colours does spot colour lithography usually print in? Tick the **two** correct options.

A One ☐ **B** Two ☐ **C** Three ☐ **D** Four ☐

Screen Printing

6 Choose the correct words from the options given to complete the following sentences.

cheap **hand** **short** **long** **expensive** **machines**

Screen printing can be done by .... or by using a variety of semi-automated .... The printing machines and the cost of producing the screens are relatively .... so the process is suitable for .... print runs.

7 When screen printing, what is used to squeeze the ink through the screen onto the paper? Tick the correct option.

A Squeezer ☐ **B** Squasher ☐ **C** Squidger ☐ **D** Squeegee ☐

8 Which of the following materials would be best for making a screen printing mesh? Tick the **two** correct options.

A Cotton ☐ **B** Silk ☐ **C** Nylon ☐ **D** Polyester ☐

Flexography and Block Printing

1 Circle the correct options in the following sentences.

a) **Screen printing / Lithography / Flexography** works on the basis that oil and water don't mix.

b) **Screen printing / Lithography / Flexography** is used in industry to print onto plastic film or carrier bags.

c) **Screen printing / Lithography / Flexography** uses a screen of nylon fabric and a cut-out paper stencil.

2 Choose the correct words from the options given to complete the following sentences.

pressed **decorative** **inked** **rolled** **copper** **neoprene** **wood**

Block printing is a very popular printing method used to print .... fabrics. It's very easy to use in schools and you can use a variety of materials as the printing surface, e.g. .... sheet. A block of materials, e.g. .... or lino is cut into. The original surface is .... and .... onto the material being printed.

Embossing

3 When is embossing used? Tick the **three** correct options.

- **A** As a surface finish to paper or card ☐
- **B** To emphasise part of a design ☐
- **C** To suggest a quality product ☐
- **D** To add colour to a card ☐
- **E** To cut out areas of the card ☐

4 What is embossing a form of? Tick the correct option.

- **A** Banging ☐
- **B** Stamping ☐
- **C** Hitting ☐
- **D** Printing ☐

AQA-style Exam Questions

Section A

Section A is about designing new products.
You are advised to spend about 30 minutes on this question.

1 Teenagers have a varied choice of body adornment. You are asked to design a product for the teenage market and give some details of how it might be manufactured.

(a) Identify three design criteria which will make your product successful with the target market. Give two reasons for each design criterion.

An example is given for you.

Design Criteria	Reasons
Should be cheap to buy	**To enable young people to be able to afford to buy it**
	To sell more products
i)	
ii)	
iii)	

(*9 marks*)

1 (b) In the space opposite and on p. 84, develop a design for your product in sufficient detail that someone would be able to make the product from your design.

Marks will be awarded for:

- (b) (i) clarity of communication (*6 marks*)
- (b) (ii) a creative response (*5 marks*)
- (b) (iii) feasibility (*4 marks*)

1 (b) (Cont.)

1 (c) Evaluate the effectiveness of your design proposal against the original design criteria you gave in part (a). The quality of your written communication will be assessed in this question.

(6 marks)

Section B

You should answer all questions in this section.
Question 2 is about materials and their properties.

You are advised to spend about 15 minutes on this question.

2 (a) Choose **three** of the products in the table.

State a main material or ingredient they are made from and list two properties of the material or ingredient that make it suitable for the product.

An example has been completed for you.

Product	Material or Ingredient	Property of Material or Ingredient
	Brass (copper / zinc alloy)	Resistant to corrosion
		Easy to cast into complex shapes
		i)
		ii)
		i)
		ii)
		i)
		ii)
		i)
		ii)

(9 marks)

AQA-style Exam Questions

2 (b) Select one of the materials from the box below.

Circle your choice.

Rice	Oak	Cotton
Aluminium	Polystyrene	Mounting board
Acrylic	Porcelain	Cheese

2 (b) (i) What is the source of the raw material?

....

.... *(1 mark)*

2 (b) (ii) Describe how the raw material is processed for manufacture into products.

....

....

....

.... *(3 marks)*

Question 3 is about packaging and environmental issues.
You are advised to spend about 20 minutes on this question.

3 (a) The disposable drinking cup shown below is claimed to be environmentally friendly.

3 (a) (i) The plastic cup has been manufactured from corn starch rather than from a traditional plastic.

Explain why corn starch has been chosen.

....

....

....

(3 marks)

3 (a) (ii) The cardboard sleeve has been made from timber grown in a **sustainable forest**.

Explain what this means.

....

....

....

(3 marks)

3 (b) The developments (nets) for the heat-proof sleeve have been arranged and printed onto corrugated cardboard sheets as shown in the diagram below.

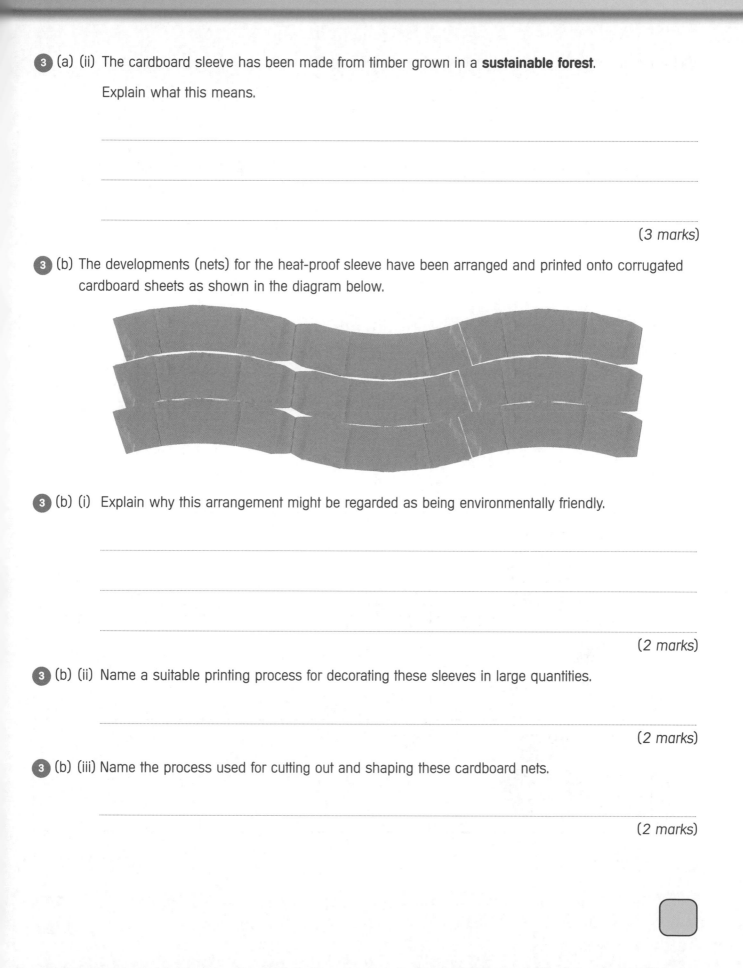

3 (b) (i) Explain why this arrangement might be regarded as being environmentally friendly.

....

....

....

(2 marks)

3 (b) (ii) Name a suitable printing process for decorating these sleeves in large quantities.

....

(2 marks)

3 (b) (iii) Name the process used for cutting out and shaping these cardboard nets.

....

(2 marks)

AQA-style Exam Questions

3 (c) Explain in detail what you understand by the term **sustainability**.

....

....

....

....

....

....

(3 marks)

3 (d) Choose two of the symbols below and explain what they mean.

Symbol	Meaning
	i) ....
2 HPPE	ii) ....
	iii) ....
x%	iv) ....

(4 marks)

Question 4 is about product manufacture.
You are advised to spend about 25 minutes on this question.

4 A local museum is promoting an exhibition of London Landmarks and would like to sell simple products with logos as souvenirs in the museum shop to promote the exhibition.

The Design and Technology Department of your school has been asked by the museum curator to design and produce 200 products with a logo, based on the theme of London Landmarks.

4 (a) Simplify the photographs into a logo to make it suitable to be manufactured in a batch of 200. You can use one of the images, or two, or all three.

Draw your design in the box below.

(4 marks)

4 (b) (i) Identify a suitable manufacturing process to make the 200 products.

(1 mark)

4 (b) (ii) Choose a material you are familiar with and explain why it is suitable for the manufacturing process you identified in part (i) and for this scale of production.

Material: *(1 mark)*

Explanation:

(3 marks)

4 (c) Use sketches and notes to explain how you would make 200 of the products using the material you have selected.

Marks will be awarded for:

- (i) accurate description of each stage of the process (*6 marks*)
- (ii) correct naming of tools and equipment (*3 marks*)
- (iii) quality of communication (*4 marks*)

4 (d) Describe how you would test to make sure your products are safe for the user.

(3 marks)

4 (e) Identify a safety rule you would follow while making your product and explain why you would follow it.

4 (e) (i) Rule:

(1 mark)

4 (e) (ii) Reason to follow the rule:

(2 marks)

Question 5 is about the use of computers in the design and manufacture of products.
You are advised to spend about 15 minutes on this question.

5 Computers have an important role in the design and manufacture of products.

5 (a) (i) What does the term CAD stand for? (1 mark)

5 (a) (ii) What does the term CAM stand for? (1 mark)

5 (b) Give two advantages of using CAD / CAM in the design and manufacture of products.

Advantage 1:

(2 marks)

Advantage 2:

(2 marks)

5 (c) Apart from CAD / CAM, explain how ICT is used in commercial manufacturing processes. Include specific examples in your answer. The quality of your written communication will be assessed in this question.

(8 marks)

This question is about smart and new materials and their use in designing and manufacturing products.

6 (a) Describe fully what is meant by the term **smart material**.

(3 marks)

(b) (i) Give one example of a smart material. (1 mark)

(ii) Describe the properties of the smart material you have named and explain how it might be used in a product.

(3 marks)

OCR-style Exam Questions

You are advised to spend 45 minutes on this section.

Fig. 1 shows a mobile phone.

Fig. 1

1 (a) Give three design features of mobile phones.

Feature 1: .... *(1 mark)*

Feature 2: .... *(1 mark)*

Feature 3: .... *(1 mark)*

(b) What are tables that include the details of adult hand sizes in millimetres known as?

....

(c) Use your own hand to answer these questions.

(i) State an appropriate length for the mobile phone in Fig.1.

....

(1 mark)

(ii) Justify your answer. ....

....

(1 mark)

(iii) Explain why making the mobile phone 110mm wide may be considered to be a design fault.

....

....

....

(2 marks)

Total: 10 marks

Fig. 2 shows a wind-up radio.

2 (a) (i) Give two reasons why wind-up radios are popular.

Reason 1: .... *(1 mark)*

Reason 2: .... *(1 mark)*

Fig. 2

(ii) Explain one drawback with wind-up radios.

....

....

.... *(2 marks)*

(b) Clockwork energy is one example of a sustainable source of energy.

State three other sustainable sources of energy.

i) .... *(1 mark)*

ii) .... *(1 mark)*

iii) .... *(1 mark)*

(c) Explain why few domestic electrical products use direct sources of sustainable energy.

....

....

....

....

....

....

.... *(4 marks)*

Total: 10 marks

OCR-style Exam Questions

3 Fig. 3 shows an iron from the 1900s and a modern-day iron.

Fig. 3:

1900s iron **Modern Iron**

(a) The modern iron has an adjustable thermostat. List three other features of a modern-day iron.

(3 marks)

(b) Explain why two of the features you have identified have made the modern iron a good product. An example has been done for you.

Example

Point 1: The iron has an adjustable thermostat.

Explanation: The temperature can be controlled so different fabrics can be successfully ironed without damage.

(i) **Point 2**:

Explanation: *(2 marks)*

(ii) **Point 3:**

Explanation: *(2 marks)*

(c) The two irons shown in Fig. 3 both have the same basic function, but their designs are very different.

Explain why the design of the iron has changed over the years.

(3 marks)

Total: 10 marks